SPORTS FOR LIFE
THE FRUITS OF PLAY & COMPETITION
For the Young and the Young At Heart

for Ise
My new awesome friend!
Jami

Bruce H. Jackson, PhD
Jami Lynn Bauer
Edited by Loren Adams

Illustrated by Merrilee A. Liddiard

The Institute of
Applied Human Excellence

www.theiahe.com

© 2010 Bruce H. Jackson & Jamie Lynn Bauer
All Rights Reserved.

No part of this publication may be reproduced, stored in a retrieval system, or transmitted, in any form or by any means, electronic, mechanical, photocopying, recording, or otherwise, without the written permission of the author.

The Institute of Applied Human Excellence
6193 West Ridge Road
Highland, UT 84003

www.theiahe.com

Published by Dog Ear Publishing
4010 W. 86th Street, Ste H
Indianapolis, IN 46268
www.dogearpublishing.net

ISBN: 978-160844-679-7

This paper is acid free and meets all ANSI standards for archival quality paper.
Printed in the United States of America

To my wife, Marta, and my sons, Blake and Lucas—
whose lives inspire me to be all that I can be.
BHJ

For my family and in loving memory of my father,
Dr. Bruce M. Bauer.
JLB

CONTENTS

First say to yourself what you would be;
and then do what you have to do.

—Epictetus

PREFACE

Sports have been a part of popular culture since even before the ancient Greeks. Within the sporting arena, contests are won and lost, and individuals and teams—from the grade school playground to the great Olympic competitions—grow from their organized physical experiences.

Beyond the thrills of victory and agonies of defeat, boys, girls, men, and women walk away from their games with more than just a score; they walk away with a new set of skills, attitudes, and qualities that can enhance and empower their abilities to reach greater heights and greater levels of personal discovery. Whether one is of high talent or of little talent, each person treads on equal ground with his or her peers, with the rights and privileges to discover who she or he currently is, as well as what she or he wants to become.

This book is for both the young and young at heart—for those individuals who wish to express themselves within and through sports and other competitive activities—hoping for greater opportunities to develop themselves in all areas of life.

For those who don't participate in the arenas we call sport, the qualities herein still apply. Each of us plays in the arenas of our lives, whether they be sports, school, work, or hobbies, or other areas of life. It is our hope that through these stories your mind will be opened to the notion that every life arena provides you with an opportunity for personal growth and self-development.

This book is dedicated to the great coaches, teachers, family, and friends whose love, wisdom, and support are immeasurable and cherished. Thank you! Special thanks go to James Arnold, Dr. Chris Barden, David Barden, Dr. Bruce Bauer, Jennifer Buntz, Darrell Danner, Dario Enriquez, Alan Fine, Doug Johnson, Dr. Zeno Johnson, Hank Jungle, Dr. James Loehr, Dr. Sharron Mathes, Bill Raymond, and Dr. Steve Wilkinson.

Many thanks also to those student-athletes who voluntarily gave their time, energy, talents, and thoughts in helping us with this book.

We also want to thank you, the reader, for your inspiration. It is your deep-seated aspirations that compelled us to write this book. May all of your hopes, dreams, and goals come true!

ALWAYS BEGIN WITH
THE END IN MIND

VISION

1

VISION

Always begin with the end in mind

There are few people who have ever achieved greatness in their lives without a clear vision. Vision is what picks you up when you're down. Vision is what motivates you to get up when you want to stay in bed. Walt Disney had a great vision, one that kept his brother and him going through financial crisis before finally making it big. But what most don't know is that before Walt Disney even started, he knew that he was going to build an empire that would entertain kids and adults alike long after he was gone. And so his vision lives on.

It is early dawn. The sun is just peaking above the horizon, and Janet, an ambitious senior with the potential to go to the state finals in the 500 and the 1000 meters, gets up for her early morning run. Day after day, week after week, Janet rises from her bed in the dark and dreary cold of winter to do what few others on the track team are willing to do—pay the price of success!

Janet discovered and crafted her image of victory last season. She had all summer to think about it, letting it sink deep within her mind. With vivid colors and clear sounds and feelings, she could see the day, hear the crowd, run the race, and feel the silky blue ribbon with the gold medallion hanging proudly around her own neck. Just last year she had seen it around the neck of her close friend who ran for another school. Janet remembered the ceremony and the way her friend climbed the three-tiered platform to the very top. It was from that point on that the road to victory was clear for Janet.

With a gap of only 2/10ths of a second, Janet knows exactly what style and technique she must master to break through to the next level of her performance. She knows what to eat, how much to sleep, how much to run, how much to dream, and how much to rehearse in her mind for this year's state tournament. More importantly, she has the picture in her mind. She sees her family and friends gathered around the final race. She knows the track, the trees that surround it, and the crowd that will fill it. The day is sunny, and the wind is blowing ever so gently. The official will be on her right and the count will be short. A round from the official's gun will be shot, signifying the beginning. This vivid movie takes only seconds to complete.

In the blink of an eye, the race is over. This year she stands fourteen inches taller at the top of the wooden platform while below her the second and third place finishers stand at ten inches and six inches respectively.

Although standing only a few inches higher than her peers, Janet knows that being number one means doing what no other athlete in her class is willing to do. With a clear image in her mind of the champion she wishes to be, Janet gets out of bed and prepares herself for the bitter cold. She looks back at her warm blankets and pillows, just begging her to come back to paradise. But Janet turns her head away from such comforts with a smile while she refreshes the vision she has so meticulously crafted since last year. Now the vision is too clear to ignore; getting back into bed would be an impossibility.

The vision is now in place: the day, the race, the other runners, the clothes she's wearing, the food she will eat prior to competition, the color of the finish line, the medal—everything. It's now just a matter of filling in the details: those morning runs, daily workouts, drills, races, rituals, and preparations for the race. Looking at the pink and steel blue morning sky, Janet knows that this is just one of many dark mornings ahead on the road to fulfilling her vision.

As Janet enters the swirling air, she notices the fresh packed snow and the smell of the burning pine from nearby chimneys. As she runs, she listens to the crunch under her feet. She begins to warm and loosen up, and in minutes she no longer feels like the elements are getting the best of her. Now she feels like the master, of both herself and of her destiny. Fatigue is now her friend. The run, the challenge, no longer controls how she thinks and feels because those things feed off the vision deep within her mind. One mile, two miles, three miles—the journey begins in her mind. Puddles are hit and destroyed, sticks are broken, sweat pours from her body, cramps once in a while, but the smile and the vision still remain because she begins with the end in mind.

Beginning with the End

Create in your mind a clear vision of who and what you want to
become, not who and what others see you as being.
It's your journey, life, and pride, not something for others to
decide. We need to begin living with the end in mind.
We ought not peer on what used to be but delight on what we
could and can be. We are such a seeking society thinking that our
ships will come in and sail safely to shore.
We need to wake up from the fantasy to face the reality that only
with wise guidance and goals will the ship endure—
We must begin living with the end in mind.
Create as an artist would, and paint a picture in your
mind of who and what you desire to be—don't be a message in a
bottle randomly thrown out to sea, for you are the
captain of your own destiny.
Begin living with the end in mind.
Let your soul be your sail and your heart's passion be the wind,
and your mind will then guide you on your journey. Let your true
desires, dreams, and goals surface to be the fuel for the fire of your
own joy and success; don't let external obstacles destroy your inner
desires, but rather, let them strengthen you so that
you can reach higher grounds.
It's time to begin living with the end in mind.
Your being needs a guide just as a symphony
needs a conductor—you can be the professor of your own class . . .
your favorite instructor.
It sounds trivial, but it's crucial to begin living with the end in
mind. See yourself as you'd like to be, paint a picture and sculpt
your thoughts for success and happiness. Be the Picasso, the reason for the rhyme, the strong oak tree grown from a mere seed.
It's true that you are the artist of your own self-portrait, so use all
of the colors, tools, visions, and dreams to create a masterpiece.
Begin now, with courage, strength, and vision for your
life time . . .
begin living with the end in mind.

© Jami Lynn Bauer

Shoot your goals to the moon and even if they fall, they will land among the stars!
—Courtney Kolb, eighth grade

Don't just reach your goals, aim above them.
—Grant Deckwood, eighth grade

You seldom get what you go after unless you know in advance what you want.
—Maurice Switzer

My thoughts on vision

THERE IS NOTHING MORE POWERFUL
THAN JUST GOING FOR IT

PROACTIVITY

2

PROACTIVITY

There is nothing more powerful than just going for it

Proactivity means to take action. This is key to your success, because if you do not take action, actions will take you. Before you can succeed at anything, you must begin the journey. Your journey begins wherever you are. Once your vision is in mind, take your first step. If that step turns out to be a bad one, take another in a different direction. Remember, those who succeed in life are not just the lucky ones; they are the ones who take the most actions. Most millionaires have lost all of their money several times before they have hit the jackpot. Remember, even Babe Ruth struck out six out of ten times at bat, and he was the "Sultan of Swat," the most popular baseball player of all time!

Scott was not an ordinary seventeen year old. He was from what many people called the "wrong part of town." His father, Mr. Schafer, was a truck driver and his mother had a part-time job at the local hospital.

Scott, their only son, was a special boy. From the time he was very young, he had been curious about everything and felt a drive to search for new experiences. As a young boy, Scott would play for hours using his imagination to compensate for his small collection of toys. He would often go out to his fifty-foot lot and dig holes, looking for new ways to stimulate his creative mind.

His parents often marveled at his ability to create something out of nothing. "He looked for opportunity everywhere," his mother said of her son. To Scott, that was just what you did when there was nothing else to do. His parents often felt bad that they couldn't afford to give Scott all the luxuries they thought other children had. Scott could often sense his parents' frustration and would console them saying, "Don't worry mom and pop, I like to create things in my mind. Sometimes it's even better than having toys." Marlyn and Jack smiled and appreciated their son's consoling nature. They were proud parents.

Although Scott was lucky to have very loving parents, he witnessed a lot of abuse among his friends' families and within his cement-laden neighborhood. There was drug abuse, physical abuse, and lots of cruel behavior. The people he lived by didn't have much money and he could never understand how they could destroy what little they had. While others he saw destroyed or corrupted much of what God had provided them, he thought to himself how important it was to cultivate what he did have. The more he saw, the more he reviled the degradation of his surroundings.

As a young boy, he vowed that he would never become a victim. He promised himself that he would never let others control and abuse him or let people or circumstances break his spirit or keep him from living his dreams.

One night during the seventh grade, after witnessing a tragic fight between two of his neighbors, he kneeled before his bed as his mother taught him and prayed that he would never again experience such things. He also made a promise to himself never to let life get the best of him or his family. He wanted to leave his old neighborhood and take his parents with him if possible—if not physically, at least spiritually. This was a big goal, he thought to himself, one that would take incredible initiative and proactivity. But that's what he was committed to do.

At the end of his prayer, Scott was inspired to write down all of the rules that he thought he wanted to live his life by. He thought this list important enough to keep with him at all times. The rules went something like this:

1. Be happy.
2. Never let other people get me down.
3. Look for opportunities everywhere.
4. Never complain.
5. Be the best I can be.
6. Take risks often.
7. Find my talents and skills by trying everything.
8. Be kind to others.
9. Never give up.
10. Never let others see me sweat.
11. Fight for what I believe is right.
12. Respect all living things.
13. Grow a little every day.

14. Take advantage of the opportunities given to me.
15. Stay healthy.
16. Stay away from drugs and harmful things.
17. Learn something everyday.
18. Be aware of my course in life and change when needed.
19. Think positively.
20. Seek to appreciate my strengths and work on weaknesses.
21. Look for the good in all things.
22. Give back to my neighborhood.
23. Help others get better.
24. Take every opportunity to grow.
25. Hug my parents everyday.
26. Obey God's laws as I understand them.

Scott read this list to himself everyday. He read it extra carefully on those days that challenged these beliefs.

School was somewhat of a breeze for Scott. He ranked at or near the top of his class at the public school he attended. Although well liked by most of his classmates, Scott had only a handful of friends whom he trusted and would spend time with. Many of the other kids got into drugs and other things that contradicted the goals he had set for himself. He often spent time alone reading and studying for his classes and occasionally painted pictures and wrote short poems about life in his neighborhood.

Despite their paltry income, Mr. and Mrs. Schaefer saw the drive and potential in their young son. Wanting to sacrifice everything they could for his development, they scraped up some money, secured a second mortgage, and made arrangements for Scott to attend Brighton Academy, the only private school within thirty miles of their home. When his parents broke the good news, Scott cried with joy and pondered the wonderful opportunity; he was one that would not take this opportunity for granted.

Although it was a tremendous learning opportunity, Scott had some tough times as he tried to fit into the elite core of boys and girls that graced Brighton's halls. But this never put Scott in a funk. He recognized this as a wonderful opportunity to learn and to grow, so he continued to pray for good friends with whom he could speak and socialize with. But more importantly, he decided to take some action outside himself.

At the end of each week, Scott would use his leftover luch money to buy an extra bus ticket to Brighton. There he would spend the day on the athletic grounds where many of the kids showed up on the weekends to play pick up games and to spend their free time.

Often he would see no one—or no one that would ask him to join in their activities. Most of the time the boys would refuse Scott when he asked to play, but sometimes odd numbers forced them to begrudgingly invite him into the game. However, whether the boys let him play or not, it never kept Scott from asking. He just kept smiling and never let what other people did or said keep him from at least trying to play. When he was refused, he would simply find other ways to amuse himself; he would pull out one of his favorite action novels, or he would watch the games and be available in case there were any injuries. Sometimes he would look for the school's janitor who was usually there on Saturday and always willing to unlock the equipment closet for him. The students called the janitor "Tiny," for his short five-feet-three-inch frame. Scott became good friends with Tiny over the course of many Saturdays. Since they were from the same neighborhood, they had lots to talk about. They just understood one another.

Just like in public school, Scott was at or near the front of the class. When the teacher asked a question, he was never afraid to raise his hand or make a contribution, regardless of any comments in the back of the room. In some subjects Scott was exceptionally talented, and where he had talent, he always took advantage of it. He would not waste even one day of his parent's hard-earned money. Scott was engaged in the moment and never let the opinions of others sway him in his desire to learn, grow, and live life to its fullest. All this said, he was still considered the outcast, the loser, and the poor kid from the city. He was called names, even threatened a few times, but Scott was above it all.

It had been several months now since Scott entered the Academy. Although excelling in most of his classes, he still struggled to put together a social life. Often as he exited the bus that took him from his subsidized neighborhood to the Academy, he watched as his classmates raced by in their Volkswagens and BMWs, often scoffing and heckling him as they went by. When this happened, Scott simply shrugged his shoulders, chuckled, and continued on his way.

It really didn't faze him until one day, Stewart, a wealthy and quite popular athlete, started pushing Scott around outside of the cafeteria patio during lunch period. Scott was in one of Stewart's classes and saw it coming, as Stewart was not one of Brighton's disciplined students. As usual, Scott ignored his foe, but Stewart had to show everybody who was boss. Stewart threw the first punch, but Scott ended the battle quickly and quietly, using only two strikes and a sweep of his leg to paste Stewart's face to the ground. It was a karate move that Scott had learned from Tiny during their many Saturdays together. (Nobody knew that Tiny had earned his black belt at the city gym.) A monitor saw what happened, quickly rushed to the scene, and escorted Stewart to the office he had seen so many times before. Word got around and the students began to form a new image of their classmate. He may not have much money or high family status, they thought, but he had something else—guts.

The first Friday of every month was dance night at Brighton, and since the school sponsored a great band, most of the students showed up, mainly just to hang out. But Scott came to dance. Unlike most of the boys, who stayed on their side of the gym, Scott was always the first to walk over to the girls' side. This astonished everyone. Although rejected most of the time—not because of his looks but because of his low social status—it didn't stop him from asking.

The asking went on and on, until finally the girls gave in. Also, they were tired of waiting for the other boys to ask them. To their surprise, he was not only a great dancer, but also lots of fun to be with and easy to talk to. Soon, once Scott took the floor, many of the girls would come out to dance by themselves. The girls were just waiting for him to ask them to dance. Of course Scott took advantage of every opportunity he saw. They would even ask him to dance at times. This in itself caused a great commotion and many other scuffles during and after school, but Scott always won; funny though, he never fought the same person twice and figured there were only so many boys at his school. Sooner or later there would be nobody left to start a fight. But until then, he continued to take every opportunity to partake of the marrow of life. Hence, his involvement in the school play.

Although quite a movie buff, Scott began developing an interest for the theater. There was not much of a program at his old school, but Brighton offered several plays during the year. Scott would often attend these plays on Saturday nights, sometimes with his parents, and sometimes alone, seeing the same play over and over again.

One day after school, he decided to poke around the theater a bit and came across a dress rehearsal for the new spring play. Scott watched for over an hour and was engrossed in the scenes that unfolded before him. As he continued to watch, he kept moving down row by row, hoping he wouldn't be noticed or kicked out. Once he hit the third row, Scott was sitting right behind the director, Mr. Mullin. Scott didn't worry anymore about being kicked out. He was enjoying himself too much. During a break in the action, Mr. Mullin introduced himself to Scott and asked him what he thought of the production so far. Scott, at first startled, was thrilled to speak to Mr. Mullin and asked several questions. Mr. Mullin was thrilled too; nobody had spent this much time asking him about all of the things he had studied throughout his life. Scott continued to watch as Mr. Mullin directed.

It was the second week of rehearsal and Mr. Mullin was trying to make the final adjustments to his cast, the costumes, and the scenes that were being developed. Mr. Mullin asked Scott what he was doing from three to five PM each day and asked if he would like to be involved in the production. It didn't take long for Scott to agree.

The very next day Scott was helping with set design and costumes and making sure that everybody was on schedule and that everything was running as Mr. Mullin wanted. During short breaks, Scott took the opportunity to speak with Mr. Mullin and learn more about the theater, its history, the plays he had been in and directed, and the running of his current show. Scott got to know the cast as well, many of which he had danced with at the Friday night dances.

Scott was well accepted in this social circle. But it just so happened that in its sixth week of rehearsal, one of the lead characters, Nathan, slipped and fell, tearing a tendon in his left knee. This threw a curve ball for Mr. Mullin, who had less than three weeks until opening night. He needed somebody, and he needed him fast. "Scott," he said with an inquisitive voice, "how about you? I've seen you dance with those girls on stage after practice. There is not a lot of singing in Nathan's part and your voice cannot be that bad. What do you say?"

Although a bit tentative, Scott took the opportunity. "Win or lose, whether I make a fool of myself or not, it's something to try, I'm sure I'll enjoy it, what the heck!" Besides a new opportunity, there was a perk involved: her name was Patty, and she was the lead.

Patty was considered one of the prettiest girls in school, and above all, very talented. She wasn't interested in most of the boys who liked her because she knew what they were after. Week after week she would get asked out by the jocks and the "in" people at the Academy, but Patty wasn't the least bit interested. Many thought of her as a bit strange. She hung out with a small group of friends and spent countless hours rehearsing. Patty was devoted to the theater and wanted more than anything to go to college in New York, where she planned to make her big dreams come true.

Patty wasn't used to such inexperience in a cast member. Even though she knew high school wasn't the "big time," she was at least used to cast members having some experience. But she had watched Scott over the several weeks. She thought him to be a genuine and thoughtful person, one that people could trust. She didn't care that he lived in a different neighborhood or didn't drive a fancy car. She was even a bit attracted to his humble background; he was different from the other boys. More importantly she respected Scott's willingness to take risks and put himself on the line, a good quality of an aspiring actor. She loved Scott's ability to endure and thought his personality quite fitting for the role he was about to play, a role of a destitute man trying to overcome the hardships of the Great Depression to court and ultimately win over the woman he loves. Scott didn't think so much about the role or even compare himself to the character; he just wanted to have fun and try something new.

Scott proved to be a wonderful partner for Patty. There were certainly a lot of mistakes made up front, but Scott always shook them off, learned from them, and kept trying. Mr. Mullin knew there would be a learning period and expected such mistakes, but he was pleasantly surprised to see the many fine talents that Scott brought to his play. Patty was also pleasantly surprised by how quickly Scott picked up on the subtleties of the art. In short, Scott was a natural. Whether he possessed the raw talent for acting or whether it was just his uncanny ability to make mistakes and to improve, Scott grew like no other student Mr. Mullin had ever seen.

Of course word got around that Scott was playing the leading role opposite Patty. This gave fuel to even more jealous boys who had yet to fight and prove themselves against the rogue from downtown. But, as usual, Scott prevailed against his aggressors, paid no attention to their childish ways, and enjoyed himself as the only guy spending two to three hours a day with the school's most desired female.

Soon, several weeks had passed, and opening night was upon them. It was 7:30 PM on a Saturday night, and the house was packed, just like every opening night. Several seats were left open for the families of the cast and crew. Scott, excited to have his parents see him, made sure that two seats were saved. He would never let the ones responsible for his great journey miss out on his theatrical debut. With only seconds before the lights faded, Mr. and Mrs. Schafer rushed in, having taken a cab all the way from the city because their car wouldn't start. As they walked down the aisle, all eyes were upon them since they were not as well dressed as the other parents. They felt a bit awkward at first, but showed confidence, like their son, as they walked to their seats. They were escorted by Todd, a freshmen who took Scott's place on the staff after he had become the big star. Todd was excited to meet Scott's parents. He too was an outsider, and he looked up to Scott as his mentor and friend.

From all accounts, it was said to be a smashing evening. A few local newspapers even came to find out about this new boy who had mysteriously made it on the Brighton theatrical scene. The play was described as having passion, romance, and a bit of reality, as the poor boy from the projects courted the wealthy girl from the suburbs.

The audience members were on the edges of their seats as Scott finally won Patty's love. As they kissed you could tell it was authentic. Just about everyone was moved—either by the emotion of love, or in the case of several senior football players, by anger and frustration. This didn't stop them, however, from respecting the boy who had done everything he could to make the most out of his experience at Brighton, allowing nothing to deter his proactive nature. And just like in the plot of the play, Scott won Patty's heart that night for real.

As Scott and the crew bowed after several encores, Scott knew he had finally won the approval of his classmates. But as he thought about it, it wasn't very important to him. He was still the same person, with the same values, core beliefs, and willingness to make his life a challenge. Scott never let life at Brighton Academy just happen to him. He was challenged by just about everybody, but it never fazed him. Whenever he got discouraged he just kept looking at his list while refocusing his energies.

Scott's beliefs and core values had brought him to this very night, to this very place in time where he and Patty, with all eyes on them, walked up the aisle amid a standing ovation. The night was theirs, and the rest of it they spent together shaking the audience's hands—even signing a few autographs.

As Scott's parents exited the theater, they were greeted with the open arms of an adoring crowd who now recognized them as the star's parents. From afar, Patty and Scott saw the scene and both smiled at his parents' joy. His parents had never experienced that much attention, and Scott had never seen them so happy.

The following Monday the same attention was thrust upon Scott. Now he was popular, had the best girl in school, and had many people who wanted to become his friend. Even those who wanted to beat him up just weeks earlier started being nice, although he did not need or want their attention. His happiness came from his ability to endure, to be himself, and to be with the girl he had fallen in love with. He did, though, get asked to play in many softball games after school, which he stayed for and enjoyed very much.

Proactivity

As you go on your way,
remember to keep a balance of work, family, friends, and play.
It's all too easy to get engrossed with work and give up on
spending time with family and friends
when they are the ones that will be there and love you in the end.
Be wise as you travel on your way;
be thankful for the gifts you've been given every day.
Don't let the negativity of the world bring you down.
Instead create your own path and let your proactivity
lead you where you want to go.
Instead of reacting to all of the negativity,
put your energy into proactivity;
make good choices, choose good friends,
and be who you truly want to be until the very end.

© Jami Lynn Bauer

Nobody can make you do anything. You have to be the source of your own power.
—Kiera Corbridge, eighth grade

You have to create your own destiny. No one else can do it for you.
—Sara Fausett, eighth grade

Of all the virtues we can learn no trait is more useful, more essential for survival, and more likely to improve the quality of life than the ability to transform adversity into an enjoyable challenge.
—Mihaly Csikszentmihalyi, author of *Flow* and world-renowned scholar

My thoughts on proactivity

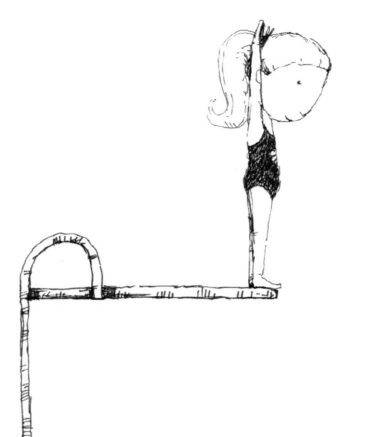

THE GREATEST REWARDS COME
WITH THE GREATEST RISKS

RISK

3

RISK

The greatest rewards come with the greatest risks

No doubt about it, without risk there is no success. Life itself is a risk. There is so much to lose and so much to gain. Those who risk learn that most fears in life are not real. For those who venture to face their fears, the world is theirs for the taking. There are too many great risk takers to single one out. You know who they are. They are the ones who ask when no one is asking and act when no one is acting. Anyone can take a risk. The question is, will you?

Sara was fourteen before her father would let her ride her bike any further than the cluttered end of Pine Drive. He also insisted that she be up at 6:00 AM and home by 9:00 PM on Saturdays. Chores upstairs, chores downstairs, mop here, dust there. Home life in "the dungeon," as Sara called it, was difficult for all of the kids, especially Sara. Her father, like some others who drank too much, rarely let any of the kids out of his sight.

Sara was the youngest of the three Delany kids. Her two brothers, Matt and Devan, ages twenty-one and twenty-three, still lived at home. Matt and Devan were both excellent students, good athletes, and accepted at several good colleges out of state, but their father convinced them not to attend any, saying it was selfish. Afraid of their father and protective of their mother, both Devan and Matt decided to hold out for a while and see if they could make a difference around the house and help out with the family income.

For most of his life, Daryl had worked odd construction jobs. Neither he nor Marge had a college education nor the money to provide that luxury for their children. Few people looked at Daryl as much more than a bum. He was often seen late at night walking the streets, filled with whatever drink the town bar had on special. According to Daryl, the circumstances of his life were always someone else's fault.

On the other end of the spectrum, Marge had been working for Butterfield's Bakery for more than ten years and was adored by all who frequented the establishment. She always greeted her customers with a smile and the breaking news of the day. "Always interested in what's going on," the head baker would say, pointing at Marge.

Marge was considered a saint, not only for putting up with Daryl for so many years, but for keeping the family together. Often, late at night, she dreamed of packing her one suitcase and walking away from her dreary situation. But because she was so dedicated to her kids, she felt obliged to remain where she was, love and raise her kids, and make the best of her marriage.

Sara's home situation repulsed her, but she kept it within the confines of the conversations she had with her mother late at night in the kitchen. When the boys were asleep, Sara would meet her mother downstairs for a late-night snack. It seemed to be the only time they could be alone together and really talk, mother to daughter. Often, under the dim yellow light of their antiquated kitchen lamp, Sara and her mother would talk into the wee hours of the morning. They would speak of just about everything and anything that crossed their minds. Topping the list were their dreams and fears.

Marge had always wanted to be in the theater, but gave up that dream when Daryl came into the picture. In her younger days, Marge had been a good student and a fairly good athlete. In the 1955 senior yearbook, she was even pegged as "Most Likely to Become a Doctor," which in those days was rare for a woman. Hwever, deep down (somewhere in her big toe) lay a pile of dreams that had never seen the light of day. Worst of all, Marge knew it.

Sara was fifteen. Now a sophmore and finally in high school, she was excited to "move up" in the world. At the same time, she was fearful because of how shy she was. She was a good student but lacked social graces and feared she wouldn't fit in. Some people thought she was kind of strange, but many of the boys felt otherwise since Sara was quite attractive. In the beginning this caused problems because she did not know what to do when a boy spoke to her. She usually greeted him and quickly thrust her head so far into her locker that there was no way of making even casual conversation. In frustration, the boys usually shook their heads and left.

Marge was no fool. She could see that her daughter was heading for the very same trap that she had fallen into some thirty-five years earlier. It pained her to see her daughter, so full of energy, become so complacent, letting her life flap in the wind while her father continued to squash her spirits with his pessimistic attitude and bossy behavior. Marge thought long and hard about what to do, but she realized that helping her daughter might force her to deal with some of her own fears. However, her love for her daughter was greater than her worst fears, and she knew she had to take the responsibility of showing Sara what it meant to break free, even if Marge was fifty-five. She needed to dig deeper and ressurect the qualities she had developed as a school girl, regardless of how long she had denied herself the freedom to be herself. She reasond, "It's never too late."

One night after dinner Marge gave Sara "the sign," which meant meet in the kitchen at midnight. It had been a while since their last talk, so Sara raised her brow and with a smile retired to her bedroom with quiet anticipation.

At midnight Sara sauntered into the kitchen and met her energetic, yet apprehensive mother. Without any hesitation, Marge blurted out, "I'm taking a class. An acting and dancing class."

"You're what?" said Sara looking like she thought her mother had gone completely mad.

"You heard me right, Sweetie. I'm taking a class, you know, at the city college."

Sara sat down in the chair next to her mother with a look of complete disbelief. "When do you start?" she asked.

"Next week. I can't wait."

"That's fantastic!" Sara put her hand on her mother's shoulder, "But, Mom, what do you think Dad will say?"

Marge's smile faltered a bit, "I don't know. I didn't ask him."

"You didn't ask him? Won't he flip?"

"I don't know, but I'm taking the class anyway!" Marge's voice raised a note as she looked at Sara. "You know, I have been serving you kids and your father for years now. I think it's time that I stepped out of my shell a bit—you know, take a risk. I could have done so many things in my teens and twenties. I think I missed out, and I'm not willing to miss out any longer. I want to live my life too."

"Well, you deserve it, Mom." Sara smiled and gave her mother a tight bear hug. "I'm proud of you."

"Thanks honey. That really means a lot to me. And I think with your support, everything will be fine."

"I'm here for you Mother. Don't you worry."

Marge looked squarely into Sara's eyes. "I'm here for you too, honey; I'm here for you too." Sara smiled.

About forty-five minutes later, the two hugged again, turned off the light, and felt their way up the staircase. Marge snuck into her bedroom, slowly raised the covers, tucked her feet into the bed, and avoided yet another marital confrontation. As she lay in bed, she thought about how her daughter reacted to her taking the class. She had seen the excitement in her eyes and knew that Sara, too, had the fire in her. "Sara's got a real chance and I've got to help her take it," thought Marge. Then she drifted off into a light sleep.

The next morning, Marge realized the commitment she had made to herself and her daughter. She hadn't actually signed up for the class yet, but knew there were still a few spots available, so she had to register quickly. Once Sara had packed her lunch and left for the day, Marge paced the kitchen. The idea of taking the class was so wonderful and freeing, yet actually doing it seemed impossible. But by gosh, she was going to do it. She was going to do it for no other reason than to model for her daughter, and the rest of her family, that it could be done and that they too could break free from their perceived life boundaries. Marge's hands were trembling and her stomach was tight with nervousness as she picked up the phone to register. Luckily, or unluckily, she grabbed the last spot.

The class took place on Monday and Wednesday nights from 6:00 PM to 8:00 PM, and today was Monday. Tonight was the big night. The first obstacle was to get past her husband. After everyone had left the house and before she left for work, Marge sheepishly looked over at Daryl and said, "Daryl, what are you doing this evening?"

"Why do you want to know?" The paper went down and Daryl looked directly at her. She twitched slightly.

Marge twisted her fingers together and fidgeted for a moment. What was she to do? After a few seconds of silence, she replied, "I'm asking because I have plans tonight, and I just wanted to let you know."

"What do you mean you have plans? You never have plans." Daryl's voice raised a few notches.

Marge steadied herself by holding onto the counter. She looked at Daryl and a sense of peace and security overwhelmed her as she

continued, "Well, tonight I have plans. In fact, I'm taking a class—
every Monday and Wednesday night."

Daryl shifted in his chair. His eyebrows narrowed, "What kind
of class are you talking about, Marge?"

"Acting!" she replied firmly.

"Acting," said her husband. "You have got to be kidding! You,
act? That's unbelievable. I think you ought to stay home with the
kids." Daryl continued reading his paper, thinking that the conversation was over.

Marge took a deep breath, looked down towards the floor, and
then pulled down Daryl's paper and looked directly into his eyes. So
far her confrontation hadn't been as bad as she'd imagined. She mus-
tered every ounce of courage she could command, and confidently
told Daryl, "You can stay home. Just for once, I would like to do
something for myself." Daryl looked in her eyes twice to see if she
was really serious, and he could see she was. Daryl backed off and
once again raised his paper. At that moment, Marge was overcome
with personal power and could hardly keep herself from smiling.

After a minute or so, as Marge began to clean the kitchen,
Daryl took one last shot at her, trying to destroy her passion, but
more importantly, her self-respect. But he failed. He was, as they
say, only a paper dragon. Once again Marge felt like she was king
of the world, at least of her own life, and she hoped that, for her
kids' sakes, they would notice. She had beaten her fear, won for
the first time in years, and finally stood up for herself. For years
she had succumbed to Daryl's threats and taught herself to be
fearful of his reactions. For years she had taken the abuse, the
constant control, and the other games that he played. And now she
had broken free. The only bad part of the situation was that it was
easier than she had thought. "Just think," she thought to herself, "all
this time wasted being afraid!"

The next night at dinner, both Devan and Matt were there for
the first time in days. Nobody knew where they had been. Daryl
stopped caring and Marge had not asked—until that night.

"So where have you boys been?" said Marge.

"Around," said Devan.

"What do you mean 'around'? From now on, you'll tell me
where you are going. If you want to live in this house, you'll live
by some rules. Now eat your supper." Marge then smiled at her two

boys. They smiled back nervously, afraid that they had crossed some unknown boundary.

Both boys were amazed, even curious about her behavior. It actually got them fired up. "Go mom!" Devan said. Matt concurred. Again, Daryl looked over while shaking his head, pretending that her newly found power was just temporary. Then Daryl just got up and left, saying he'd be out for most of the night. Everybody knew what that meant.

Since Daryl was gone, Marge let the cat out of the bag that she had just taken her first acting and dancing class. "You what?" said the boys. They too were quite amazed and now figured that the swift castigation they received might have something to do with her increased confidence. They were right. As Marge began to tell her two boys, and Sara once again, about her decision to take this class, they got more and more excited that she had found her freedom. They listened as their mother described all that she had learned, all the things she had tried, and how wonderful it was to be able to express herself like she did back in her school days. For the first time in ages, the four talked intimately with one another. They talked like a family talked. And for hours they enjoyed each other's company, the children basking in the glow of their mother's experience. They yearned for the same. Marge had done it. She had broken through, and her kids were there to witness. By the end of their long conversation, both boys seemed to have no energy for going out, they just wanted to be home. Again Sara was ecstatic and couldn't wait to get more details that night in the kitchen.

At midnight, Sara heard heavy footsteps on the stairs—no pitter patter, but thumps. She thought it must be her father, who had come home about an hour earlier. She looked around for someplace to hide, but to her surprise, Marge danced in and greeted her daughter with a big smile, like it was the middle of the day. Sara smiled back and didn't even need to ask about the flagrant disregard for silence. She saw in her mother's face something new, something invigorating and full of life.

Daryl lay upstairs in bed, staring at the ceiling after being wakened by the noise. But he did nothing about it. The steps were too sure, too confident.

For hours that night, Marge filled her daughter with the wonderful experiences she'd had in class. She told Sara about all the people she had met and practiced with, just like she had done so many years earlier in high school. Sara soaked up every detail. As the evening went by, both women laughed and cried together. They laughed because of joy, and they cried because of the fear they had let themselves experience for so long. When they finally decided to retire at 4:00 AM, Sara was filled with her mother's spirit.

The next day, Marge was once again reciting lines while dancing around the house. Earlier that morning, she had been hit by the most astounding news: both her boys were registering for college and moving out. They both had earned enough for a full year's tuition and rent, and it was time for them to go. Finally, she thought. Then, grinning from ear to ear, she saw something from the corner of her eye. It was Sara walking up the driveway, and next to her was a young man, and a very good looking young man at that. As they entered the house, a very surprised mother looked at her daughter who could hardly wait to introduce her new friend. "Mother, I'd like you to meet David." Both women looked at one another and, without a signal, knew that this was yet another night to meet in the kitchen.

The Delaney house on Pine Drive was never the same again. All because of taking a little risk!

Trial and Error

How do we learn if we're not willing to try,
How can we live in fear of our lives?
So often we feel uncertain, that we might fail—
we feel so timid, so rigid, so frail.
We must be willing to let down our guards,
just allow things to happen without trying so hard.
We must reach forward and look beyond the terror,
we must live and learn through trial and error.
Push forward, look ahead, and
break through life's many barriers—
That will indeed take courage and strength . . .
that will definitely entail many trials and errors.

Love,
Only Human

© Jami Lynn Bauer

You must feel the fear and do it anyway.
—Shannon Ditsen, age 13

I had a lot of paper dragons. One day I slew one. That was a great day.
—Ben Olson, age 14

The greatest danger for most of us is not that our aim is too high and we miss it but that it is too low and we reach it.
—Michelangelo (1475–1564)

My thoughts on risk

SOMETIMES YOU JUST
HAVE TO LET GO
_____
TRUST

4

TRUST

Sometimes you just have to let go

To trust oneself is to let go. To trust another is to believe that they will not do you wrong. In your life you will have many coaches. Some will be from sports, and others may come in the form of teachers, or even bosses. The sooner you learn to trust in yourself and others, the sooner you will tap into powerful resources that will take you to greater heights.

Oh my gosh!" cried Kyle as his ball landed a good foot outside of his opponent's doubles line.

"Kyle, now come on. You can do it," whispered his dad through the fence, next to the sign that read, "Mountain Heights Junior Regional Tennis Tournament."

Kyle, with tense shoulders and a furrowed brow, hit his next two shots long and slammed his racket on the ground. It was all downhill from there. The second set was filled with unforced errors, poor shotmaking, and an even worse attitude.

After the match and tournament were over, Kyle walked with his dad through the country club and past his friends, still analyzing the match in his mind.

"I can't believe I'm hitting wide again," he told his dad. "What's wrong with me? Maybe I need to turn my body more or keep my eyes on the ball—or maybe follow through better. If I could just focus on everything . . ."

His father interrupted, "Hey Kyle, don't analyze so much. You did fine, and remember it's only your first year on the junior circuit."

"But dad, I got sweeped!"

As they passed the club's weight room, Kyle saw the club pro working with a young player on stretching and prematch routines. Kyle stood there and watched.

"Hey, Dad!" Kyle said. "I've seen that guy before. He's worked with a lot of the top juniors on the circuit. Maybe he could help me too. What do you say?"

Kyle's father, Martin, thought to himself for a moment. He thought back over the last few years as he introduced his son to the game while taking the family to their athletic club. Of all the sports he had introduced Kyle to, tennis was the only one that stuck. Kyle dropped everything else because of pure frustration, too much thinking, and anxiety. This was just like him and his friends in the science club. They had to understand everything—leaving nothing to mystery or instinct. Every problem had to have an answer and, unfortunately, this philosophy permeated everything his son did. But he did have to give his son credit; this was the farthest Kyle had come in any sport. And therefore he would do anything to support him. Weighing the opportunities versus the risks, he happily granted the request. "Well, I suppose there's only so much I can do with you. Let's go and have a word with the coach."

The next Saturday morning was Kyle's first official lesson. Kyle and tennis pro Steve Anderson entered one of the back courts with a bucket of new tennis balls. After introductions and a brief conversation about Kyle's background, Steve was ready to see what he could do with his new protégé.

"Now Kyle, we've got thirty minutes to work on your tennis. What do you want out of our time together?"

"To become a great tennis player!"

"Let's start with something a little more specific."

"Okay then, how about my forehand."

"All right, that's better. Let's get out on the court and hit a few."

"But hold it, you're the professional here. Aren't you going to show me what I should be doing, you know, like the pro's?

"Well, you know Kyle, every pro is a little different. There's no one right way to hit the ball. We have to work with your style and body. We have to develop a game that's right for you."

"I just want the formula, coach."

Steve handed Kyle a few tennis balls and pointed towards his side of the court. "Just remember, there's only the ball, the court, and you. Let's see if we can discover what your formula is. Now why don't we start by hitting some balls crosscourt."

Kyle went to the baseline and swung away at the balls Steve was feeding him. He missed only three shots out of ten.

"Seventy percent. Not bad," Steve said as they met up at the net.

"What are you talking about? Half of those seven were off by a long shot. My shoulders aren't sideways, and I'm not moving my feet. What do you mean not bad? There are a million things going wrong." Instead of giving Kyle specific instructions, Coach Anderson simply asked his student if he could just focus on when the ball hit the ground and when the ball hit the racket. Thinking this would be easy, Kyle spent the next fifteen minutes hitting balls. Steve would hit them randomly, and Kyle would yell out "bounce" every time the ball hit the ground and "hit" whenever the ball hit the racket. After several minutes of doing this, there was less talking, more focusing, and more balls going over the net. This was an odd experience for Kyle.

After all the balls were gone, Steve asked Kyle to pick them up in silence. After all the balls were picked up, Steve shook his hand, and said he would like to see him next week. "What a strange lesson!" Kyle thought to himself.

Before leaving the court, Kyle turned back to his new coach and yelled: "I'll be practicing my crosscourt shot all week."

"Fine, but try not to analyze so much," retorted Steve. "Focus on your target and leave the rest alone."

This just didn't make sense to Kyle. "How can anyone get better by not thinking about it?" thought Kyle to himself. Then curious, he walked back towards his coach, scratching his head. "It seems like I should be focusing on my shoulders, feet, and stance. Those are the things that are causing trouble for me, aren't they?"

Steve sighed. "Just hit the ball, Kyle. I promise you it'll come."

"I'll try," said Kyle. And off he went.

The school week felt short—especially in chemistry, where Kyle and his buddies skipped lunch to crunch numbers, study chemical models and mix compounds. It thrilled Kyle and his friends to analyze experiments and understand the underlying properties. One afternoon Kyle was at his locker gathering his books before he went home for the day when out of the corner of his eye, he saw Murial, one of the cutest girls in his junior class. He was staring at her when she glanced back at him. Both quickly turned away pretending not to notice the other. Tim, Kyle's best friend and leader of the science club, saw what was going on and came over to check out the situation.

"Kyle . . . I saw her look at you. Now why don't you go over there and talk to her—maybe ask her out?

"I don't know. What if she blows me off?"

"Then she says no and she walks. No biggie."

"I'll tell you what will happen. If I actually make it to her locker without tripping, she won't know my name. Then if I actually talk to her, the whole time she'll be thinking, 'How did I get stuck with this guy talking to me. I hope no one sees us.' I won't be able to say anything interesting or even close to funny. Then she'll tell her friends about Kyle, the geek, and I'll be the laughing stock of the school."

"No you won't. Nobody is going to care except me, of course. Get it out of your head and pull yourself together, man. Murial is awesome. I might even ask her out myself if you keep this up."

"Don't even think about it."

Murial glanced at the boys again as she shut her locker, clicked the lock, and walked away.

"Man, you are something. You gotta take life by the horns, bro. Just be yourself; go for it, and see what happens. Win, lose, or draw, at least try to connect with her."

"I know . . . I know."

Later that evening, back on the court with Steve, Kyle swung away and continued to analyze his every mistake.

"What am I doing wrong, Steve? I'm trying to keep my shoulders sideways, my knees bent, and swing low to high, but my wrist is doing something funny. I can't quite get it."

"Well, what are we trying to accomplish here?"

"I'm trying to hit the ball down the line as close to the cone at possible."

"Okay, so when you do that what do you notice?"

"What do you mean, what do I notice? I notice that my shoulders aren't sideways, my knees aren't bending, and that I'm raising my racket too much on the follow-through."

"What if you forgot about those things for a while," asked Steve.

"But that's tennis," howled Kyle.

"Forget about those things for a minute."

"Then what would I think about?"

"How about nothing?"

"How do I become better if I don't think about something?"

"Have a seat, Kyle."

"Sure." The two walked over to the bleachers at the edge of the court.

"Tell me, Kyle, are you a good student?"

"Yes, I'm in the top five percent of my class."

"Let me guess, you like to analyze things don't you?"

"Yeah."

"Got to understand the why behind everything, huh?"

"I haven't really noticed. I guess I do. In school for sure, well, for most of my classes anyway, and a lot when I'm with people. I mean, sometimes with girls and stuff."

"Girls—yeah they're tough not to think about, especially when you like one?"

"That's for sure!" Given the look on his face, Steve had a hunch that there was something behind this statement. Steve thought for a minute, then had an idea.

"Kyle, do you want to become a better tennis player, I mean really break some barriers?"

"Of course I want to break barriers: I'd also like to make the varsity team this year."

"Really!"

"Yeah, really!"

Are you willing to do whatever I say and ask no questions?"

"That would be tough. I like to ask questions."

"Does that mean you don't want to do it?"

Kyle fingered the strings on his racket and thought about his coach's question. "What's in it for me?"

"How about peace of mind, trust in yourself, definitely a better tennis game, and maybe even a good time."

"Well, all right," he said. "If you think it will help, I'll give it a shot." Kyle rubbed the back of his neck and thought to himself, "What's all this going to accomplish?" He quickly caught himself and stopped his natural chain of questioning thoughts.

"First things first," said Steve. "So what's the name of the girl you've been meaning to talk to?"

Shocked that he knew, under his breath Kyle said, "Murial." Now he knew he was in trouble. "Again with the thinking," he thought.

"Great. I want you to promise me something. Tomorrow, before the end of the day, you have to say hello to Murial." Kyle was still. "Will you do it?"

"But what if I get rejected? What if she thinks I'm a geek? I'll tell you what will happen. After one minute, she'll make an excuse that she has to leave. Then she'll tell her friends all about it. They'll laugh at me, and then . . ."

"Whoa, whoa, whoa," Steve interrupted. "What did we just discuss? Will you do it or not. You have to trust me here Kyle."

"Okay, okay, I'll do it." Another lesson ended.

The next day Kyle woke with butterflies in his stomach, and he wasn't even at school yet. He'd never had butterflies like these before. "These are butterflies of a person about to get beat up," he thought to himself, before remembering to stop his negative thoughts.

Right before first period, he told Tim about the "big plan."

"I'm behind you all the way, bud." Tim said. "But if you screw up, I'm going in myself." This angered Kyle just enough to turn his butterflies into determination. That's what Tim wanted for his friend. And it worked.

By the end of fourth period, American Civ, Kyle felt sick to his stomach. He usually dozed off in this class, but today he was pumped up for the encounter. "This is crazy," he thought. "What's Steve trying to do to me? I'm dying here," again came his untrusting thoughts. Then he thought about all of the kids Steve had helped get college scholarships. He was always getting calls from his former students, getting thanks for all he had done. "He knows what he's talking about. I've got to trust him," Kyle decided. When the bell rang, he knew it was time.

Tim was near Kyle's locker, just waiting for the big move. Others close by had heard through the grapevine that something might happen next hour, so there were more kids than usual down the back hall next to their lockers.

"You look sick, man."

"Get out of here. You might as well grab a bag of popcorn and a lawn chair, you're being so obvious," Kyle said, giving Tim a light shove. Tim laughed as he walked over to take position at the drinking fountain.

Murial was right on time. Her blond hair was full of curls, and her green shirt was the exact shade of her eyes.

"Oh man, she had to look so good today of all days," Kyle thought. "I can't believe this. What if she laughs in my face? What if everybody watches me get dogged? What if . . ." But Kyle knew he'd made a promise, to his coach and himself. And deep down, Kyle believed in both. There was no way of backing out now.

Murial opened her locker and glanced towards Kyle's locker. She then planted her head in her locker and began looking for something, or pretended to look for something anyway. Once Murial ducked her head into the locker, Tim quickly waved Kyle towards Murial.

Queasiness turned into to full-blown nausea as Kyle began to walk sheepishly in her direction. Now within five feet, his heart started thumping like a drum. He tapped her shoulder with a shaky hand. She looked up at him and smiled.

"Hey Murial, I'm Kyle."

"I know your name. And that's your buddy over there, Tim. Right?"

"Yeah, how did you know?"

"I see you looking over here. I always wonder what you guys talk about."

Not really knowing what to say Kyle blurted: "Probably you, I guess."

Murial laughed. "Well, it's about time you stopped over, then."

With the weight of the world lifted, Kyle smiled back. After a few moments of bliss, he couldn't help but notice a short saying taped to Murial's locker door:

Sitting quietly, doing nothing
The spring comes and the grass
Grows all by itself.

"What's this?" Kyle asked, touching the green leaf border.

"Just a short quote I picked up in my Asian history class. Do you like it?"

"I don't know. I'm not sure I get it."

"I guess it means we should let go of ourselves and watch the world do its thing."

"Very interesting," replied Kyle, just standing there thinking.

"Hey, Kyle, it was really nice to talk with you, but I've got to run. I've got a lab to finish before tomorrow. Stop by again, okay?"

Kyle nodded. "See you later," he called to Murial. And it was over just like that. Everyone near the fountain clapped as Kyle walked back proudly to his side of the hallway.

Still smiling, Kyle walked toward Tim.

"Right on, Kyle." Tim slapped a strong hand on his shoulder. "You are the man."

"Wow, thanks, Tim," said Kyle as he reviewed the incident in his mind once again. However, something else stuck in his mind. It wasn't just Murial's green eyes, cute voice, and sweet smile. It was that silly little quote taped to her locker. He couldn't stop thinking about it. Then he finally got it.

"You really don't have to mess with nature for it to work. In fact, most things happen without any understanding at all. I guess not everything can be controlled by this advanced society of ours," Kyle thought to himself.

Throughout Kyle's next class, he thought about all the things that don't require any control at all, such as the weather, gravity, the makeup of a molecule. He began to realize that there are greater forces in the world than just human beings. In a way this comforted Kyle. He had never realized how powerless he was to change, to control, to manipulate certain things. This reminded him of Steve's council that didn't make much sense before. Now he was getting it.

The next day Kyle returned to the country club and the first thing he did was tell Steve about his big day. "I was scared out of my tree," he said. "What if she had blown me off?"

"Did she?" asked Steve.

"Well, no, but she could have."

"So what if she had. There's nothing you could have done about it anyway. Kind of like your tennis game, isn't it?" Steve said. Kyle thought for a second about the quote in Murial's locker.

"So do you think you can take the same risk with your tennis?" Steve asked as they approached the court.

"What do you mean?"

"Do you think you can let go long enough to let your body just hit the ball?"

"I don't know. I suppose it's time to try."

"Great, now get over there and let's try it out. And again, no thinking!"

During ten or so shots, Kyle obsessed with trying to correct his swing, his knees, his shoulders, and other parts of his game.

"Kyle, Kyle," Steve stopped him midswing. "Quiet your mind. No judgment, no talking, and no frustrated looks. Agreed?"

"Agreed."

"All right. Now, what's your target?"

"Crosscourt on the forehand side."

"Now that you have a goal in mind, I want you to do one simple thing. When you see the ball bounce, say bounce. When you hit the ball, say hit. That's it."

"Again with the bounce-hit?" asked Kyle.

"Yes, again with the bounce-hit!" Now let's get to it."

After a few shots, and to Kyle's surprise, his stroke began to take shape, and like at his first lesson, he hit more balls in the court in twenty minutes than he usually hit before in one hour. He was letting his body do what it already knew how to do. Better than that, he was letting go. Finally he began to trust in his own skills and ability to hit the ball. He was in a state of flow. And it was awesome.

The next day after chemistry class, Kyle slipped away from his friendly discussions with his science buddies and aimlessly walked back to his locker, not thinking about much, which was cool. Tim had not yet arrived, and Murial just happened to make an early stop at her locker. Without hesitation or restraint, Kyle scooted over until once again he could see the poem taped to her locker:

> Sitting quietly doing nothing,
> The spring comes and the grass
> Grows all by itself.

He smiled and his question slipped out naturall,. "Hey, Murial, would you like to go out Saturday night?" As the words left his mouth, Kyle realized that her answer did not really matter.

Trust

As we travel through this life,
a word stays with us, stands so strong and proud.
A word that echoes throughout our minds and
hearts, a word with much validity.
Believing in yourself without doubting,
putting stock in yourself without questioning.
To walk with your head high and shoulders square.
To look at life with both eyes open and alert.
A wonder, a miracle, a joyous thing our life is—
do we continue to question when we know the answer is
inside us? Or do we look into the mirror, smile, and
say things are ok?
To understand and seek knowledge is encouraged—
to continue to doubt what you are is to
slowly wither away your precious life.
The word that must be thought of with high regard,
the word that you must believe in and use as much
as the sky is blue and the stars twinkle up above—
the word is within you,
let it soar high like an eagle in flight
yell, shout, or chant it if you must—
carry it with you daily
say it with me now . . .
trust!

© Jami Lynn Bauer

No trust, no freedom. No freedom, no fun.
—Steven Jensen, eighth grade

Put your trust in God and nothing can go wrong.
—Eliza Sanders, junior high student

If you can't trust yourself, who can you trust?
—Bruce H. Jackson

My thoughts on trust

IT'S YOURS TO EARN

CONFIDENCE

5

CONFIDENCE

It's yours to earn

Developing your confidence is one of the most important things you can do. Confidence is something that is not given to you, but earned through consistent effort and determination. It comes from experiencing the small victories as well as the large. Whether you are an athlete or not, you must make the most of each of your successes. Write them down whenever you can, and remember your best performances. They will sustain you through the bad times. Remember, confidence begins and ends with you. You are the master of your own fate, the captain of your own ship.

Just as at every meet, Kate was shaking like a leaf on a tree. Staring from the waiting deck and looking down, she could see the gates dotting the snowy hill below. Before stepping up to ski, she tried to rehearse the run in her mind. She practiced mentally how she would shift her body weight and maneuver her skis, but once again she was interrupted by the crowd of people who were watching from the hillside, cheering for her and her teammates. "I just have to make it through this course," she told herself.

"Kate Neeley, you're up!" the race coordinator called. Kate curled her toes in her ski boots and tightened the straps around her gloves for the fifth time. She then moved into starting position. With tense muscles, she listened to the countdown: Three . . . Two . . . One . . . Go! Her arms propelled her body through the gate, and suddenly she was flying. At 5.4 seconds into the run, Kate could see the mass of people out of the corner of her eye, as well as her rival skiing just behind her. The pressure began to mount. Her thoughts seemed unstoppable: "What if I fall today? What will everybody think of me if I lose to this girl? What will Coach Peters think? My school? Mom and Dad? If I fall, will it cost us the race?"

Suddenly, Kate caught her left ski by one-half of an inch on gate seven. Her body twisted and dropped against the slope. As she slid towards the fence, she could see and hear disappointment all around her. Heads dropped, and the crowd hushed as her competitor soon raced through the finish line. Kate slid to a stop, while Melanie, her closest friend, ran from across the hill to check on her.

"Are you hurt, Kate?" she asked.

"No" said Kate as she lifted her body off the snow, her spirit still in agony. Today was one of only a few opportunities she and her team had to be selected to compete in the national championship, and the opportunity may have been lost. It was yet another disappointment.

Like most dedicated athletes, Kate was always eager to improve herself. She rose early, ran her five miles, then hit the weight room before going to school. She was the first to arrive at practice and last to leave.

Kate was considered not only dedicated and gifted, but also afraid, but at what? People didn't understand her.

At times, Kate demonstrated almost world-class abilities, and her coaches were excited to work with her talents, hoping to create an Olympic champion. But rarely were there two meets in a row in which Kate performed well. She had few problems with solo runs or with untimed runs. Kate could knock almost a second off any run if the clock or other athletes weren't running against her. But just about any activity that required performing against someone or something frightened her. The others girls on the team tried to support her, encourage her, and make her feel safe when performing, but nothing seemed to help. This scared and frustrated her and everyone around her, including her parents.

Despite the other girls' attempts to include her, Kate didn't have many friends. She was nice, fun to talk to, and pleasant to be around, but usually only in close and personal conversation. The group thing just didn't work for her. She didn't know what to say, how to act, or how to blend in. Whenever one of her friends or teammates did get her to go to a party or gathering, she complained that she was always self-conscious and never very comfortable. She often spoke out-of-turn, jumped into conversations too late, or fumbled her way through a group activity. At the end of the evening, she always left frustrated and disgusted with herself. She was trying too hard. The worst part of these experiences was watching others effortlessly weave in and out of conversations, participate in activities, and generally fit in.

Kate often talked to the school counselor about her social problems as well as her problems at home. Kate's father was a well-known executive and always on the road. Her mother was gone almost as much, spending most of her time in volunteer work. Kate, her two sisters, and her brother always had conflicting schedules. They didn't often meet at the dinner table; holidays were the only time they really spent together.

Unlike most of the other girls at her school, Kate grew up quite well-to-do. This was reflected in her clothes, her manners, and her "very independent" family. Most of the kids thought of her as being too good for them. She, on the other hand, thought they were too good for her, so both sides kept to themselves. Occasionally Kate ate lunch with a group of skiers, but only if they invited her. For the most part, the other kids didn't understand her, so they left her alone. In light of her circumstances, Kate, with all her talents, was a bit uncomfortable with the world around her.

In life, it seems that opposites show up almost everywhere we look. Where there is light there is dark, where there is sweet there is usually bitter, and where there is good, evil is not far away. By contrasting, each opposite seems to define or clarify the other. This sometimes happens with people as well. This is what happened when Kate met Tara.

It was another Friday lunch hour, and Kate, as usual, was alone in the corner of the cafeteria, reading a favorite romance novel. None of the team came by today, so she dug right into the juicy parts of the book. After only five minutes and three pages of the second chapter, Kate felt a tap on her shoulder.

"May I sit with you?" The words came from a tall, thin girl with long, curly black hair clinging to an unfamiliar face. Not knowing quite what to do, Kate politely offered the stranger a chair.

"I'm Tara," the girl stuck out her hand in Kate's direction. "I just moved here from Michigan."

Kate responded, "I'm Kate," then just listened.

"I'm getting used to meeting people," Tara told Kate as she pulled a sandwich out of her brown bag. This is my seventh move in the last eight years."

"You've moved seven times?" Kate shut her book. "How come?"

"My dad's in the military."

"Really! What's it like."

"Well, we've moved a lot, but I've met a lot of people and seen many places. It's been a lot of fun—tough sometimes, but a lot of fun. My brothers and I have experienced a lot together. I guess that's why we're so close. But now they're not here, they're in college. It's just me and my parents 'cus I'm the only one left." She grinned. "I get all the attention now."

"You're so lucky," Kate sighed. "I wish my family and I were that close." Just then the noon bell rang, signaling the end of the lunch hour. Kate and Tara looked at each other in surprise; the time had gone by so fast! They had so much left to talk about that they decided to meet that evening at the mall—after ski practice of course.

The two new friends met at the mall in Kate's new Jetta and decided to start at REI where racks of discounted ski shirts and sweaters where lined up.

"Do you want to look here?" Tara asked.

"No, I get all the ski stuff I need from the team—and a few sponsors."

"Are you that good?"

"I don't know," Kate confessed. "My coaches think I have some hidden 'talent.' But I often don't know where it is. But, ever since I watched the 1980 Olympic Games on TV as a kid, I've always thought I could ski like that. My coaches say that I could ski at that level, but I don't know if I believe them anymore."

"Why not?"

"Because I've spent so much time training, and I still haven't been able to break through. I don't think I have what it takes, and plus, I choke all the time. I guess I'm just afraid."

"Kate, if everyone thinks you're this awesome skier, what's keeping you back. I mean what's there to be afraid of?" asked Tara.

"Not everyone thinks I'm awesome. Once I overheard my dad tell my mom that he didn't want me to grow up a loser like his brother's kids. Ever since I was little, he's always been a real stickler for winning and being the best."

Tara stopped shifting clothes around the rack. "I think that's a bunch of bull, Kate—you know it, and I know it. You know, that's most of your problem. You let yourself believe that junk. Nobody knows more about you than you, and only you can make the choice to believe anything. Let me ask you, do you want to be the winner everybody talks about?"

"Of course. I'd do anything to find out how good I could be."

"Anything?"

"Anything," replied Kate.

"Well, one of the things I learned growing up is that confidence comes in little pieces at a time. It's not something you have or don't have, it's something you develop. You know it's really been scary for me to make new friends at every new school I've been to. I've had to learn to be outgoing. I was never that way before."

"You mean you used to be scared? I can't believe that," said Kate.

Tara shrugged. "It's true."

"Well, then how did you become so outgoing?"

"Lots of practice. Yep, lots of practice," Tara said as she put some clothes she'd been fiddling with back on the rack. In fact, let's not shop anymore, let's practice developing a little confidence ourselves, shall we." Tara took her friend by the hand and led her into the rest of the mall.

"Okay, let's get to work. So what are you most afraid of?" asked Tara.

"Mostly people, I guess. I mean, I don't really know what people think of me, and that's hard to handle at times."

"Well, so what kind of people get to you the most."

"People I've never talked to before, or people that don't know me."

"That wasn't the case with me, now was it?"

"Not really, that's because you came up to me. We might have never met if you didn't do that."

"All right then, do you see that old lady sitting on the bench over there? Go ask her what time it is."

"Why?"

"Just walk over there and ask her if she knows what time it is. That's not so hard. Come on, go for it. This is the easy stuff. Come on, it's an old lady for crying out loud." Kate reluctantly walked over to the lady and did, in fact, inquire about the time. But the only answer she received was, "Don't you wear a watch young lady?"

"Yes, well, sometimes. But mine is broken," Kate said with a still shaky voice.

"Then why are you wearing it?"

"Uh, I don't know. Habit, I guess." Kate looked toward Tara, pleading with her eyes for Tara to rescue her. Tara shook her head and motioned with her hand for Kate to stick it out. Finally, the old lady reached for her spectacles.

"It's seven-thirty dear," she said.

"Thank you" said Kate, as she ran off back towards Tara.

"Now that wasn't so bad, was it," said Tara, recognizing that it was probably a lot harder than it looked.

"A little awkward, but not a big deal," replied Kate.

Tara decided then to give her friend a little more to chew on. At that moment their attentions were drawn to a boy across the room—a very good-looking boy in fact. Kate saw Tara's glance, and quickly shook her head. She grabbed Tara's arm, trying to pull her out of the store.

"Don't even think about it," she whispered. "Not in a million years!"

"Just go over and say hello to him," Tara said, while pulling Kate back into the store.

"Kate, listen to me for a second. If there's one thing I learned in my years of moving from city to city, it's that there are lots of things that you can't control. Sometimes you've just got to look a situation in the face and just deal with it—see it as an opportunity. That's what's given me confidence. Now it's time for you. Just like difficult races, just accept the difficulty and just go for it. I look for these situations all the time. Each time I have a breakthrough, and I feel a little bit better about myself, more confident, and definitely more free. It's the greatest feeling in the whole world. The rewards of the risk are always worth the effort. Even the smallest risks have given me tons of confidence. On the other hand, when I give up and let fear control me, I feel terrible, weak, and out of control."

"You mean you actually felt those things too?"

"All the time."

Kate paused. "I thought I was the only one who went through this stuff."

"Hardly, everyone goes through it. It's just the winners who go for it even when they are scared. Remember, it's not about the out-come or about winning and losing like your father says. It's about being yourself and finding out who you are and what you're made of so you can be free."

"I just figured that when I can rid myself of fear, then I'll be able to make the change."

"No, no, no!" You can't wait for the fear to leave. Confidence comes from feeling the fear and doing it anyway. I go through the same thing every time I want to talk to a boy."

"I guess you're right," said Kate. She took a deep breath. "I just never thought of it that way. I hope I don't freak out."

"You won't," Tara said as she gave her an encouraging nod. She could feel Kate start to shake.

Before she could think too much about it, Kate walked toward the boy and began picking through the clothes on the same rack that he was looking at. She felt moisture on her palms from her nerves and tried to look busy—consumed in thought. After thirty seconds Kate's nerves really started to get to her. Finally, she looked up. She didn't know what to do. The boy just looked at her. "I have to say something," she thought to herself.

"Hi," Kate said, bracing herself for rejection.

"What's up?" replied the boy with a look of interest. Kate could hardly believe it.

"Not much. Just looking for a ski jacket," replied Kate. The boy looked down in frustration—Kate started to panic. "He thinks I'm weird," she thought.

"I just can't find my size in here," he said. After a few moments of searching, he grinned at her and headed off into another section of the store.

It didn't matter whether the boy actually had to go or whether he had blown her off. She did it! Kate was grinning from ear to ear as she approached Tara.

"You were great, Kate! The next time it'll be even easier."

While still at the mall, Kate went up to three other boys and made the same attempt at conversation. Although nothing really came of it in terms of getting phone numbers or dates, she didn't really care. Previously, she never could get herself to come close to boys; now she was walking right up to them, asking them questions, and even making conversation with them. By the end of the evening, the fear and shaking had almost stopped. The process of meeting boys was so much fun.

When Kate and Tara finally left the mall, Kate was beaming. She looked over at her friend and said, "You know. I feel good, I mean really good."

Tara thought, "Let's see if we can do this with her skiing."

Inspired that night, Kate decided to write down a list of all the obstacles in her life. She trimmed down this list into just three categories: conversations with her dad, fear of competition, and relationships with her classmates. With this brief but critical list of "paper dragons," she vowed to overcome her fears and find peace in herself.

The following week, Kate managed to confront her father and the problems she was having with his high expectations. She also participated in three conversations with people at school and even was asked to be part of a study group. These mini successes gave Kate the confidence she needed.

In the car on the way to the slopes for the last race of the year, Kate visualized herself breaking through her paper dragons on the ski slopes. She pictured herself focusing on the gates, tightening her body at each turn, and crossing the finish line without worrying about anything or anybody else. She practiced feeling the fear and pushing it away; she felt the pressure but continued to focus; she saw the people, but kept on skiing. As she continued to see these wonderful pictures, she knew that nothing could keep her from doing her very best. By repeatedly practicing what she wanted to do, Kate began to realize that no matter what happened, the world wasn't going to fall apart.

Kate tightened her clasp on her poles and listened to the countdown once again. "Three . . . Two . . . One . . . Go!" Kate kicked out of the gate. She flew through gate one, then two. She focused on the next gate and nothing else. She could hear calls and shouting from the crowd, but she let them slip quietly by her, focusing instead on tightening her body at the turn of the gates, just like she had pictured in her mind while in the car. Kate could feel the sting of the wind against her face and the speed of her body as she leaned into the curve on the final gate. As she flew by the gate, she could see the finish line. Moving even closer towards her goal, she felt the pressure, but she propelled her body anyway and smiled. "Win or lose," she thought, "it doesn't matter." Crossing through the finish line, she saw her father waving at her, cheering. Now, looking at the clock was only a formality. Her race was over. Either way, she was confident.

Self-Belief

One heart, one soul, an ever-striving
individual with many goals—
So much talent and support,
Many who believe in you and the various
things you pursue . . .
Is that enough to carry you through?
To have friends, family, and believers
is just one facet of your make.
It's all quite simple yet so complex—
what does it really take?
It all starts within—it starts with you
and ends with you;
It's a realization of reality and dreams . . .
It all starts with self-belief.

Love,
I believe

© Jami Lynn Bauer

There is an I in confidence!
—Alex Seydow, junior high student

Confidence is not taught, it's earned.
—Terry S., high school student, Hopkins, Minnesota

You've got to take initiative and play your game. Confidence makes the difference.
—Chris Evert

My thoughts on confidence

SUCCESS: IT IS NOT ALWAYS
ABOUT TALENT

PERSISTENCE

6

PERSISTENCE

Success: It is not always about talent

Most success comes with great sacrifice. Very few of us will get something for nothing. Being the best we can be comes from putting in the time, doing the work, and learning from our experiences. Thomas Edison is one person who exemplified persistence. After more than five thousand tries to create the electric light bulb, he finally found the formula. When asked in the middle of his experiments how he was dealing with so much failure, he simply replied that he had successfully tried thousands of formulas that did not work. Essentially he was getting closer each day to success. This is what persistence is all about, and it is critical in your sport and in your life.

Since he was five years old, Todd had dreamed of playing football. Every Monday night, Todd, his brothers, and his father would gather in the living room to watch whatever game was on TV. Disgusted as always, the female side of the Mitchell family usually went out for ice cream or huddled in the kitchen to discuss new concoctions for next Sunday's postchurch meal.

Todd's interests went way beyond football. He was also a gifted student with an outgoing personality. His teachers always commented on his drive and willingness to do extra work or stay after class to get something more from his teachers. His extracurricular activities also demonstrated his outgoing personality.

Not much of a partier, Todd spent most of his weekend nights with friends, playing cards, talking about all the girls they had yet to ask out, and rattling off football statistics.

Within his group of friends, who were often considered the nerds or brains of the school, Todd was the only one who actually had a chance of making the football team, or any nonacademic team for that matter.

Although his school life was on track, there was something missing. Todd had a burning desire to play football, despite his lanky 125-pound frame. This was ninth grade, and Todd knew that there were two special things about being a ninth grader. First, it was his last year in the junior leagues of academia, and second, he was eligible to try out for the Williams High School football team.

On the first day of tryouts, Todd came in as a no-name-just-a-number, not knowing anyone. Tryouts were, of course, brutal. He had heard all the stories, like the kid who broke his leg during his first day, or the unfortunate jock strap incident that took place in the showers. Although intimidated, Todd was up for the challenge.

Blocking and tackling were only half his worries. The head and assistant coaches took each prospective team member aside and tested their speed, agility, strength, and overall athletic ability. Although Todd was quite fast and agile, he was smaller and weaker than most of the other boys. But this didn't stop him from doing his best in every test he took. In fact, because of Todd's apparent desire to succeed, which was obvious from the minute he walked onto the field, the coaches worked him extra hard, even until he lost his lunch. This didn't bother Todd. He cleared his mouth and started bouncing on his feet once again. "Bring it on Coach," he yelled. It was his way of saying he was ready for whatever they could dish out.

Despite his dedication and drive during tryouts, Todd did not make the cut. Coach's words kept playing over and over in his head, "I'm sorry Todd. We can only keep so many. Maybe next year." Over and over he thought about these words, not to get depressed over, but to make the day even sweeter when he did make the team.

Instead of feeling sorry for himself, Todd checked the coaches' office hours and sat down with each to get advice on how to acquire the skills and strength necessary to make the team next year. With several suggestions and a list of accompanying short-term goals, Todd ventured off to become something more, somebody stronger, somebody better.

Starting the next day, Todd began visiting the weight room three times a week. He ran, swam, and went to every football game he could. He showed up at practice to watch, learn, and take notes. He approached the game much like he approached academics—with a goal, a sense of passion, and a clear plan.

During and after his ninth-grade year, Todd gained almost twenty pounds from his combination of multiple protein and vitamin fortified shakes. Summer included stacking lumber at the local yard, attending football camp, and playing lots of social football with his friends. Todd and his friends just couldn't get enough. Although no varsity letter graced his jacket, Todd proved himself to be the best of the bunch. But he wasn't satisfied; he had yet to earn his varsity letter! After all, being tagged by 110-pound geeks with thin white arms and coke-bottle glasses hardly felt like being on the Williams' front line.

Tenth grade finally arrived, and fall tryouts were once again gruesome. But this time, Todd knew where to go, where to change, which players to beat, and which kids he could now intimidate—if just a little. He, like everyone else, could easily tell the rookies from the veterans by their bent-over positions and the traces of vomit on their helmets after two dozen sprints and countless push-ups. Todd was ready this year. Two weeks before tryouts he had prepared an even more grueling and disciplined workout regime. This time he was right with 'em.

On the first day of tryouts, Todd looked around and didn't feel so small anymore. Although still not large, he retained his quickness while improving his endurance and proved to his coaches that he could block with the rest of the team. This year the coaches took notice.

As Todd came off the field from blocking and tackling some of the biggest players on the varsity team, Coach Walters and Assistant Coach Petersen took him aside and congratulated him on his improvement and persistence.

When tryouts concluded, each man waited with anticipation for the results of their days' trials. After several minutes of congratulations to those whose names were called, Todd became more nervous, and rightfully so. His name wasn't called. Coach Walters called Todd, dejected and sorrowful, over to the sidelines.

"Todd Mitchell, may I see you for a moment?"

"Yes, sir." Todd practically knocked over Coach Walters as he ran to receive his long-awaited message.

"Todd, I've seen few young athletes as dedicated as you. Your improvement from last year is impressive, but not as impressive as your willingness to come out here and tough it out. This is difficult to say, but I'm sorry, I cannot give you a starting spot on this team. However, you show more persistence and determination than most of our star players, and for this quality we would like to invite you to practice with the team and teach these guys how to work and be dedicated. And if, in fact, we get stuck on the field and you're ready, we may play you; but that's no promise."

As Coach Walters completed this statement, he looked into Todd's eyes and gave him a warm smile. Todd didn't know what to think. He wasn't officially on the team. He hadn't reached his goal, but nevertheless, he was a part of the team.

After a few seconds, Todd honorably accepted his coach's invitation. In addition, Todd looked right into Coach Walter's eyes and said, "But remember this, I will make this team. Whatever it takes, I will make it!" No look could have been so serious, so intense, so absolute. Coach Walters concurred with a nod and knew his pledge was a sincere one. Despite his current weight, height, and ability, Todd would eventually make this team.

Practices came and went. Todd suited up for every practice and every game and even traveled with them to out-of-town games, studying and keeping up with his homework on the way. Todd was a machine during practice. Although he usually took quite a beating, he was always willing to get back up and take it one more time. In fact, he worked so hard that some of the players began to resent him. Coach often referred to Todd as an exemplary member of their team. This angered the players, and many were jealous. However, each also understood the concept that they were only as strong as the weakest link. Though he was smaller than the rest, no member of the team could claim that he was that link.

Todd gave it his all that season. He lifted with the team, ate with the team, and even socialized with the team. Todd had gained their respect—and a little weight—but most of all he had gained their friendship. Some even coached Todd, giving him tips on diet and things he could do to put on the mass he needed to compete with the bigger players. The only thing that Todd did not get was a starting spot on the team, and this fact still burned in his chest.

Another year came and went. Todd, like the rest of the team, gained more experience, more skill, and a few more cuts and bruises. Although most of his friends looked the same, Todd had a more streamlined body and a more defined face. His eyes reflected confidence and he was more relaxed. His close friends, sisters, brothers, mom, and dad all noticed something different. More important, Todd noticed. Although this change was apparent to himself and those close to him, he had something left to prove—not to his friends or his family, but to himself. He still had to earn a letter for his varsity jacket.

It was now the first day of summer vacation after his junior year. Todd woke up, flopped onto his side, and thought to himself, "Another summer." Most of his friends relished the beating sun, warm beaches, nights of laughing conversation, and talk of dreams after high school. But Todd, although not without goals in other areas of his life, had but one real passion. Two years of his education and football had gone by, and his most important goal had not yet been reached. He had spent all last summer with a powerful visionand that was to make the Williams team. That year came and went. Of course he was proud of his dedication, loyalty, and commitment to the team. Even with the physical and often mental abuse, he was happy to be there. Still, he was left without peace and contentment.

"Is it worth it?" he thought to himself. "Can I really do it?" As he continued to lie in bed, Todd felt he had a choice to make. Should he repeat another summer of camp and early morning workouts? Was it all over, or was it the eleventh hour when the real test would be given? For the very first time, Todd fell to his knees and started to pray with all his heart. Todd poured out every thought and feeling that was running through his mind for his maker to hear. He wanted an answer.

After a few moments he quieted down and cleared his mind. With that came a very strong impression: "Finish what you have started." Immediately after, another thought entered: "You don't want this. You're wasting your time getting your butt kicked for nothing." "Finish what you have started . . . butt kicked . . . finish . . . butt . . . finish . . . finish . . . finish." It wasn't so much the words as it was a feeling, a feeling of what it might be like to look back and wonder if he could have made it, with just one year left. Todd imagined himself ten years into the future, sitting at a desk somewhere, thinking back to a time when he was struggling to make a team, to achieve something great.

His heart sank for a moment. "Is this what I want to look back and see? All that work to give up now?" he wondered. "I've got nothing to lose unless I don't try." Todd began to shake. His energy level increased. He got up, flopped onto a small couch and thought about everything he had been through since his freshmen year—the tryouts, the practices, the training, and the time. Few were as intent as he was to reach his goal. Quitting now would stay with him for the rest of his life. He thought to himself, "Even if I never make the team, I'm much better than I was last year, both as an athlete and a person." He was right. Everything he had done, every thought he had formed, every action he had taken, and every choice he had made changed him from the inside out. He felt good about himself. He wasn't ready to throw in the towel—not for himself, and not for the team.

Todd jumped from his couch, grabbed the phone, and called Coach Walters.

Coach Walters' wife answered the phone. Greetings were exchanged, and then Coach, after coming in from the backyard, answered the phone.

"Hello."

"Coach Walters, this is Todd, Todd Mitchell. Do you have a minute?"

"Sure, Todd, what's on your mind?"

"Coach, I've been busting my butt for two years now, and I haven't made the varsity squad. Part of me wants to give up on this game, but I know I can't. Can you help me. I mean, can you give me some suggestions on what I can do to be varsity material?"

"I'll tell you what, Todd. Come on over to my house tomorrow morning and we'll talk."

"Really? That's great Coach. I'll be there early."

Coach Walters laughed. "I'll see you here at 7:00 AM sharp then."

"Thanks, Coach." When Todd hung up the phone, he felt good about his decision.

The next morning Todd was at Coach Walters' house by 6:50 AM, waiting on the front porch. Coach Walters opened the door at 7:00 AM, invited Todd in and right away put him to work. In exchange for work in his yard and garden, Coach Walters spent countless hours teaching Todd everything he knew about football, even the secrets that helped him get his scholarship and all-American honors at Notre Dame. He told him things that Todd had never heard before, things that few of the athletes knew well.

He even lent Todd some of his most prized books on strategy. In exchange for work around the house, Todd gained one of the best educations of his high school career. Coach Walters even learned a few things himself from his young protégé.

Along with Coach Walters' training, Todd returned to football camp and made everybody take notice. He was now 165 pounds. He was quicker, more agile, and at least thirty percent stronger than last season. He wasn't considered a runt any more. He was considered a possibility.

Todd continued his training with Coach Walters throughout the summer, although there were several half-days where coach had to leave and Todd was left to tend his yard. He also began an even more intense workout schedule that dealt specifically with balancing technique and physical ability. Todd had become a balanced player, athlete, and person, someone that understood how the many parts of his game and life somehow came together to produce an even greater whole. This was more than Todd ever thought he could learn from practicing football, and he had his coach to thank for his newly found wisdom.

By the end of the summer, Coach Walters had the nicest yard in the whole town, and Todd was on fire. Williams' precamp had started, and each of the coaches, after speaking with Coach Walters, had asked Todd to be there. Now a senior, Todd didn't look at his teammates in awe. He knew them and they knew him. He was hit by them, and now was his chance to hit back.

After so much work and so many hours of training, what Todd lacked in size and ability, he made up in technique, raw determination, and his more balanced approach to training. Todd was becoming an all-around athlete to the extent that Mr. Watkins, the men's track coach, tried to recruit Todd. He thought about the letter that might finally grace his jacket, but it was football, and football only, where he would finish what he started.

Football tryouts were as grueling as always. Not only were the players better, but the coaches were as well. Coach Walters had spent much of his summer afternoons meeting coaches from other schools. Todd often wondered why his summer practices with Coach Walters were cut short or split into shorter sessions. Now he knew. Coach Walters was leaving.

One day before tryouts began, Coach Walters felt compelled to answer the questioning looks from the players, especially from Todd. He gathered the men together.

"You may be wondering why there are so many new coaches among you. Well, I want you all to know that next week I will be stepping down as head coach of Williams High School football."

With this said, jaws dropped and many gasped in disbelief.

Coach Walters continued. "You know I've coached this team for fifteen years. I've listened to your dreams, watched you grow, and sent many to the finest universities in the country. Well, I have had a few dreams of my own over the last couple of years, and one of those dreams is to coach college football. I've always loved the game. I loved playing it, and I've really loved coaching it. And this has been my true love, coaching. For these fifteen years I've not only taught wonderful young men this game and the lessons behind it, but I've also been pursuing my graduate degree in education. I'm now close to finishing that degree, and just last week, after years of study and persistence, I was offered a teaching and coaching position at my alma mater.

"I'm going to miss you kids. You've been my hopes and my dreams. I see a lot of me in you, especially young Todd over there, whom I've worked with over the summer months. You, Jimmy, Dan, Pete, and Trent, all of you have been my inspirations. We all come from some uncertain and insecure place. Each of us fight within ourselves to be what we have decided is important to us. Todd told me just a few months ago that he wanted to make this team. Many of you know Todd's story, yet nothing has kept him from doing whatever it took to be here. And here he is today ready to get his butt kicked one more time to get closer to his dream. That's a rare commodity, fellas. All of you in some way have persisted. If you hadn't, I would never have let you on this team. All of you have that special something that makes you one of the finest football teams in the nation.

"I am no different than you. I've always had a dream and a goal of coaching university ball. Now I have my chance. Since my acceptance, I've done a lot of thinking about this team and about each of you. I want you to know that nothing feels better than to see someone or something grow. And that's what I've seen in this team.

"Now you have a choice to make today. What are you going to do, and how are you going to play? Let me tell you that we have a very gifted group of coaches here, some of the finest in the country. They've agreed to work with you to see for themselves what this team is made of and if they want to be a part of it when I'm gone. You should be honored.

"Now it's time for us to see what you're made of. Everything that I am, I have put into this team. Show me and these coaches what you've learned, and make me proud. It's your moment of truth. Now let's get to work!"

"Yeaaaaaaaaaaaah! Go, go, go, go, go, go." The boys almost trampled each other. The energy, the excitement, the dedication they displayed were part of a philosophy, a mission. Todd, like the others, proudly displayed his tears when he hit the cage. He was awesome, they were awesome, and the coaches were thrilled.

Coach Walters was pulling for Todd today, but Todd's fate was out of his mentor's hands. The coaches were engaged at every moment, giving their attention to every player on that field. Coach Walters stood by and watched as they passed by Todd, watching, noticing, not acting as if he was a star or a straggler, but like he was just one of the players that belonged on the field. He hit, he spun, he ran, he blocked. There was no more in-your-face talk with Todd. No more shakes of the head, no more subtle rejection from the seniors. Todd was on track. Todd was a football player.

At the end of the day, the scene was as predictable as it had been the last three years. A few looked dejected. Some were on the sidelines bent over. Others were talking with their friends, and the rest were intent on knowing if their names would be called, if they would be given a number only they could wear.

Todd was a little bit on edge, as you could imagine. After tryouts were over, he just lay down and looked up at the sky. He thought about his lifelong dream of becoming a football player. He sifted through his years of struggle and hope. His senses were dull as he played the movie of his past in his mind. He heard nothing. The blue sky looked like a tunnel. The images of this movie raced back and forth in his mind.

While Todd lay in a trance on the ground, the coaches compared notes and discussed who they were going to keep—and who they were not going to keep. Coach Walters listened intently to each of the visiting coach's comments and allowed each to judge based on his own criteria. This had never been done before in Williams High School football, and Coach Walters was quite proud of this idea. He felt maybe his newly earned degree had something to do with it.

Upon completion of the coaches' meeting, Coach Walters took the coveted list and began calling names. Todd, although still staring into space, began to pay attention. Several minutes went by. Several names were called. Todd's was not among them. It was all over.

"Huddle up," said Coach Walters for the last time at Williams High School tryouts. Todd looked up and stared into the face of his buddy Brian. Brian had started on last year's team and was one of Todd's mentors. Brian looked as upset as the rest of the players, who looked at Todd in disbelief. The group gathered around Coach Walters.

"I know some of you are less than satisfied about today's results, and you ought to be. Some of you weren't good enough, and that is hard to live with. But these are the times that define who you are and what you're made of. Are you going to go home and quit because of it, or are you going to learn from your mistakes, get better and stronger, then try it again?"

Those newcomers whose names were not called learned their first lesson from Coach Walters. Many lifted their chins as their expressions moved from discouragement to determination. They all knew there was one among them who had spent the past three years learning and trying again. Someone who, until today, had never given up. Then Coach continued.

"I have just one more thing left to say. We're all wondering why Mr. Mitchell's name has not been called. Well, there's a reason for that, and I have a few things left to say". Todd shifted his weight and glanced at his feet as the men looked in his direction. "Three years ago Todd came to this field and got his butt kicked, much like several of you today," Coach continued. "Did he walk away and quit? No he did not. He found new ways of improving his game and he came back bigger, stronger, faster, and more skilled the next year. Then last year he failed to make the team once again. In fact, many of us coaches looked at each other and said, 'Here's a kid with all the persistence and heart in the world. But he just ain't gonna make this team.' But what did Mr. Mitchell do? He kept working, harder and harder, smarter and smarter. He even called me up in the middle of the summer and asked me for help. I admire what he did. I admired him, so I helped him. I took time out of my schedule, and my thesis, I might add, to work with this young man. And do you know what? He became a better football player, probably the most dedicated and persistent player I have ever seen." At this point Coach Walter's voice was a little shaky. "With all that said and with all the feedback I have received from today's coaching staff, I wanted Todd's name to be the very last name I called to play on this team. So it is my honor to name Todd Mitchell as the newest member of the Williams High School varsity football team."

With the last announcement, the whole team roared with joy while Todd stood in amazement. His dream had finally come true. He couldn't feel anything except the fourteen young men heaving him into the air. From his new eight-foot perspective, the only thing Todd could see was the sky. Todd was the varsity football player he had always wanted to be, and he would hold this moment in his heart for the rest of his life.

Persistence

What is it when you've been knocked down
not once or twice but
again and again and again
then once more—
Do you stay where you lay or stand up,
wipe off the dirt, patch the wounds
then walk forward knowing that the more
you've been knocked down the
stronger you grow, the more you learn . . .
you continue to walk proud—you persevere.
What is it when you've been told
"no way, never, you can't."
You hold your chin up high and say with pride,
"I can, I will, the challenge is my friend,
my companion till the end."
What is it when you have a dream so grand
and wondrous that you decide to journey towards it,
you achieve your heart's desire;
A small idea, into a big idea, into goals,
then a dream come true.
What is it when you can do anything you
put your mind to while others say you cannot?
That's persistence!

© Jami Lynn Bauer

Persistence is going through a rough time and coming out with a great reward.
—Luke Pesonen, junior high student, Hopkins, Minnesota

It's amazing what I can accomplish if I just don't give up.
—Taylor Wood, age 14, Oak Canyon Junior High, Utah

Satisfaction lies in the effort, not in the attainment.
Full effort is full victory.
—Mahatma Gandhi

My thoughts on persistence

IT'S REALLY UP TO YOU

ATTITUDE

7

ATTITUDE

It's really up to you

"Attitude isn't everything, it is the only thing." You've heard this said time and time again, and it's often true. No matter what happens to you, how you choose to think about your current situation is purely up to you. Attitude is like the weather of your mind. You can either make it rain or you can make it shine. It's totally up to you. But one thing is for certain: without a positive attitude you'll either fall short of your dreams, or you'll be a miserable success.

Like every day after practice, Chuck placed his secondhand racket into its case and gathered all of the tennis balls that he and his team had hit during practice. Using this time for self-reflection, Chuck usually thought to himself about his strengths and weaknesses as well as new strategies for improving his game. So focused on improving the game, he heard nothing.

"Hey, Chuck!" yelled Seth, the number one player on the team. "Are you leaving?" After a long delay Chuck looked up.

"I suppose," said Chuck. "I'd like to stay and get some extra time with Coach, but my dad needs me to help fix the tractor, so I gotta go. Seems a rod was thrown or something."

"Are you headed up to the parking lot?" Not giving Chuck time to answer, he continued, "Great, I'll walk with you."

Like everyone else on the team, Seth liked being around Chuck. There was something about him. Part of it was his easygoing nature, his simple philosophy of life on and off the court. Others just fed off his positive attitude, his passion, and his energy.

Soon there were others walking along side the pair. As Chuck, Seth, and the boys walked through the soccer field and towards the parking lot, Seth, as on most days, was down and out about his game, and like usual, needed a bit of a pep talk.

With Seth it was always something. On one day it might be the wind, another day his racket or some other thing beyond his control. Although his complaining got old, Chuck was patient and happy to listen to his talented friend complain about tennis, school, or any other subject that he might bring up.

Chuck listened intently to his problems, then, like always, tried to leave his friend with some words of advice and a way of looking at his problems differently than he had before. You might say that Chuck was a bit of a counselor to Seth and the other boys on the team.

"Seth, let me remind you that you are the best player on this team, if not one of the best players in the state. Can't you see that your perspective is a bit flawed?"

"Not really," said Seth.

"Well, no matter what you say about yourself, I and the rest of the team really admire your talent. It's fun to watch you play. You know there's really nothing wrong with you. You just need to learn to think differently about yourself. Do that and you will behave differently; do that and you will get different results from what you are getting now. That's as simple as my philosophy gets."

Seth shrugged, and after several moments of walking towards his car, looked up only to comment that tomorrow would probably bring rain.

"I wonder what can help this kid. Whatever it is, it's got to be bigger than his negative attitude," thought Chuck.

By this time, the boys had reached their cars. Seth pulled out the keys to his Mustang while Chuck struggled to open the door of his father's '74 Chevy pickup. Chuck couldn't help but notice that the Mustang was new.

"That's a nice car you've got there, Seth," Chuck said taking a closer look.

"Thanks. My dad bought it for me last week. It's an okay ride. My brother's the lucky one; he got the Audi. This car doesn't handle as well in bad weather as my brother's car." Once again, Chuck just shook his head.

"I'll see you at the match tomorrow," said Chuck, waving good-bye to his negative friend.

"Yeah, if it's not raining,"

After school the next day, Seth arrived just before his match, but an hour late for the warm-up. Of course, the first person he looked for was Chuck. It seemed that everybody liked to warm up with Chuck. Even though he was just barely off the junior varsity list, he brought something special to the team. After Seth arrived, the opposing team's busses showed up, and tons of kids piled out, ready for action. After some brief introductions by Coach Wilson and a short warm-up, the matches started.

After two hours, Chuck was in the third set of his match, and he was trailing—just barely. Between games, he took long drinks of water, gathered his energy, and focused his attention on what he needed to do before he stepped back onto the court. It was his turn to serve. Chuck bounced the ball a few times, tossed the ball into the air and smashed it into his opponent's court. Ace! Chuck smiled and pumped his fist. The sweat was dripping from his forehead onto the ground. That extra practice time was paying off. By this time most of the team had completed their matches. Half had won and half had lost. Andy, Will, Matt, Vinny, Dave, and Morse all came to watch Chuck pull out another impossible win. While watching the impossible take place once again, they threw a few cheers towards Carter and Seth's court, realizing that they would probably have little trouble beating their opponents. Twenty minutes later, after a few gutsy crosscourt shots and some fancy footwork, Chuck roared with enthusiasm and raised his racket in the air. He had once again clawed his way to victory.

Meanwhile on court one, Seth was in his third set as well, and he wasn't at all happy about it. Seeing his frustration, Coach came over between games to see what he could do with his gloomy number-one player.

"What's the problem, Seth?" he asked. Seth just nodded.

"You can beat this guy. You're three times better than him."

"I know, I know, but I'm stinking up the place. My strings are loose and it's so darned hot. There's no shade over here. Look at Carter over there; he's cool as a cucumber."

"All right, knock it off," Coach interrupted. "Just try to focus. We need your win." Coach turned and walked away from the fence frustrated, pondering what he could do to help his best player grow up and take responsibility for himself.

Seth's complaining increased, and within minutes, his meager crowd began to dwindle. Now there was no shade. Once his crowd left, Seth lost his cool, his attitude, and his match. "He seemed to give up on himself after the first set," noticed one observer standing next to the coach. Luckily, Chuck's match (at the last varsity position) carried Bloomfield High to victory.

After eight such contests, Bloomfield once again clinched the conference title. Thanks to everyone except Seth, who won less than half his matches, the team was still headed back to the state tournament.

It had been a long season and the Bloomfield Cougars were quite lucky to make the state tournament. Everyone had worked hard and kept the team spirit high—everyone except Seth, who continued his negative comments to himself and others. Up until this point, Coach Wilson had tried to be as understanding as he could. He knew that Seth, while getting everything he wanted from his parents, did have his fair share of problems at home. It was because of this knowledge that Coach cut him so much slack. But it was now time for the state tournament, and he wanted nothing to get in the way of everybody else's success. Besides, it wasn't fair to the team. Knowing that Chuck had some influence over the team, even Seth, Coach Wilson had an idea. This was the last practice before their big day so he gathered the players together for a team meeting. Once in a huddle, he looked over at Chuck and the rest of the team and asked if Chuck wouldn't mind giving the team a personal thought before their great challenge. He thought that Chuck's drive, attitude, and enthusiasm for the game, despite his mediocre talent, might keep the fire alive.

Over the past month Chuck's attitude had spread and it showed. Others had been staying late at practice to play and drill. Even when Chuck couldn't stay late, others did, often staying until sunset. From the coach's recollection, this had never happened before in his coaching career. There was a new energy. Chuck, of all people—the last on the ladder—had set the example, an example that influenced the whole team.

Accepting Coach's request, Chuck stood in the middle of the group, looked each of his teammates in the eye, and told them how much they meant to him. He told them how much it meant to be part of the team, and that he would do everything in his power to help each of them reach their goals, on or off the court. Mostly, he just wanted to say thanks for accepting him, knowing that there were others on the team that were far more gifted than he was.

"You all know that it's not because of talent that I'm on this team. I guess I'm here for other reasons. I like to work hard, I believe in myself, and I believe in my teammates. Most of all, I believe in our ability to work hard, improve, and become better athletes and people. This isn't just a sport. It's a way for us to tell the world who we are, who we want to be, and what we will do to become successful."

"For me, tennis is a metaphor for life. I may not ever win a tournament or play as well as any of you, but I can tell you this. No one will ever call me a quitter, lazy, negative, or a loser. No! I'm out here to find out what I'm made of so at the end of the season or at the end of high school I can stand proud and leave here better than when I came. I invite you, my teammates, to do the same."

It was a touching and inspiring moment for everyone. It was the first time any of his teammates saw the connections between their game, their attitude, and their lives.

After his personal thought, a few hugs, and a heartfelt reply from Chuck's teammates, Coach announced the lineup for the state championship. Chuck held his breath. He had worked hard to earn a full-time spot on the varsity team since he usually played on the junior varsity; being on the tournament squad meant he would finally earn his varsity letter.

"Andy and Will, I have you at first doubles; Carter and Matt, second doubles; and Dave and Vinny, third doubles. As for singles: Morse, you'll play number one." Coach Wilson paused and looked up. Seth's jaw dropped and his scowl could hardly be hidden. Morse was his arch rival. Coach continued as the two top players stared at each other. "Seth, you'll play number two; Joey, three; and Chuck, four. All the others will stay on junior varsity and will be there to cheer us on at State." Chuck's face split into a wide grin. It was a dream come true. He received congratulations from the team, looked at the courts, picked up his racket, and headed back to the courts where he would do what he always did: work hard, focus on his game, and support his teammates. Now was the time to make another dream come true.

That Friday, the team and their friends and families sat waiting for the tournament to get under way. It had been raining all night, and the courts were covered with puddles. A frustrated Seth sat under the covered stands, complaining about the rain and how it was going to throw off his game. Under a large tree, Chuck sat thinking through his strategy while visualizing his way through the tournament. Most of his teammates followed suit and prepared for their matches with high hopes and positive attitudes. Finally, at about one o'clock, the sun peeked out from behind the clouds, and the courts began to dry. Tension took the place of the rain, and Coach Wilson began pacing around the courts, studying his players and their opponents. This was a single-elimination tournament with just eight teams and three rounds: two rounds on Friday, and the final round on Saturday. After an hour of anticipation, it was finally time to play ball.

The first round of the tournament was almost too easy; Bloomfield breezed through thanks to Morse and Seth (who miraculously got into his groove early), as well as all of the doubles teams, who won in straight sets. The second round wasn't so easy. This time it was closer. Morse was down a set, but through raw determination came back to win three. Seth began to crumble under the pressure, once again making excuses, embarrassing himself, and really stinking up the place. Hearing Seth from the other courts, everyone else began to struggle as well. The energy level of the team was dropping, and nobody had an easy win. Luckily, through sheer determination and remembering what Chuck had talked about at the team meeting just a few days before, Bloomfield managed to clear the second round by just one match. To their amazement, they were headed for the state finals.

As with every state final, hundreds of fans showed up Saturday morning to witness the battle. Moms and dads crammed into the stands and wandered the courts to get a glimpse of their sons and daughters. Coach Wilson stood in the bright morning sun, gathering his players together for one last short conference.

"Men," he said. "I'm going to be blunt here. Our opponent is St. Peter's, last year's state champs. They're full of talented athletes, and they've made it to this final without much opposition for three years in a row. If we want to beat them, we have to play our best games ever. And, more than anything," Coach Wilson paused and looked at Seth, "our heads, and more importantly our attitudes, are going to determine the outcome of this state final. Remember what it took to get us here. Remember how we fought, how we worked together, and how hard we've worked to be the most positive and hard working team in the state. You all should be proud of your efforts and your sacrifice. A special thanks to Chuck for his words and acts of encouragement over the past few weeks. Now it's time to take that energy and enthusiasm and put it into every match today. You've done it before, now do it again—every one of you!" Coach Wilson looked once again at Seth. "Now go out there, do your best, and decide who you want to be today!"

An hour and a half into the match, Coach Wilson's troops were down. Carter and Matt had won, but Dave and Vinny and Andy and Will had lost. Coach Wilson kept his hopes up. They were still just three matches away from the state title. But it was still a long ways away.

Chuck wiped the sweat off his forehead and took a long swig from his water bottle. He and his opponent were tied. Each had a set and now it was 6–6 in the third set. His match now depended on this tiebreaker game. Chuck poured some of his water over his head and let his body completely relax for a short time. He searched for his parents on the packed bleachers and saw his mother's tense and worried expression. Chuck waved at her and smiled, trying to lighten the atmosphere. He felt calm inside, sure that his hours of practice would pay off; plus, he had built so much confidence in himself throughout the season—he knew he could do it. It was just a matter of time and focus. He may not be the best player out there, but he sure could outlast anybody mentally—and physically for that matter. When his five minutes were up, Chuck jumped up and bounced on his toes. He returned to the court still smiling. As he repeated to himself how strong his serve-return was, Chuck could feel the burst of energy surge through his arm and his racket, sending the ball cross-court and out of his opponent's reach.

"All right!" Chuck roared with enthusiasm. He started bouncing on the balls of his feet again and stepped back to receive the next serve, focusing on the fun of the moment. You could tell he wasn't about to lose.

Coach Wilson turned away from watching Chuck's match, confident in the outcome, and went looking for Seth. Upon arrival on one of the last courts (this was a bad sign), Seth looked down. Right then Carter ran over to mention that Morse had just lost.

Seth now was taking his five-minute break before his third and final set of the tournament. Seth was strong in his first set, but was going downhill fast. He won only two games in the second set, and to all watching, the match was over. Given the circumstances, if his opponent was to win the third set, Seth and his team would kiss the first-place trophy good-bye.

Unlike Chuck, Seth sat slumped in the corner of the court with his head down, elbows propped up on his knees, and his hands holding his head. Coach thought to himself that Seth looked rather pathetic. At the same time, he saw Chuck come jogging over to Seth's court, where the rest of the team stood in anticipation.

"Good match, Chuck," Coach said. "That was some of the best tennis I've seen yet from you—once again your fighting spirit and attitude carried you through. Now how about jump-starting Seth out there?"

"Yeah, it looks like he could use a good swift kick in the rear."

Coach shook his head. "Just look at him. He's lost it again. He really needs you Chuck. No, we all need you. Why don't you go talk to him—see what you can do."

Chuck walked across the court and sat down next to Seth. Everybody was watching.

"Hey, Seth. So what's going on here? What's the matter?"

Seth took his hands away from his eyes and glared at Chuck. "What do you mean what's the matter? What's not the matter? I'm getting stomped on . . . Did you win?"

"Yea, but Joey lost. That means it's all up to you. If you win, we all win. If you lose, we all lose."

"Great, just great" said Seth to Chuck.

"Hey, listen. The only thing that matters is if you play your heart out. You wimp out and give up and everybody's upset. If you do your best and give it your all, then everyone will think that you are a winner—even if we lose. It's time to choose who you want to be Seth. Do you want to be a winner or a loser? Either way you will have to live with that choice for the rest of your life." Seth pondered a moment and then looked up towards the sky.

"Now listen to me. I saw the end of your last set. This guy is getting sloppy. He's not expecting anything from you. He obviously hasn't seen the Seth that I know. He hasn't seen the state-ranked Seth Donaldson. You know that Seth, don't you . . . don't you?"

Seth looked up. "Yeah, I've met him," he said with a smile. "I haven't seen him in a while though—a long while."

"You know who he is and you know how he plays. Now the choice is yours. I'm looking at the guy who can dish up 120 mile per hour serves. I'm looking at the guy who made it to the national tournament. I'm looking at the guy who took a set off a professional player. Do you know that Seth? Do you? I certainly do. Remember how you felt during those times? Remember when you played and felt your very best. Remember all of the wins? And do you remember the positive and upbeat attitude you had during those times? Do you see what I'm talking about here—can you see it?"

"Yes, I can see it. I can even feel it a little."

"Great, then do what you feel is right and keep the images in your head."

Seth started to nod his head slightly. His eyes narrowed and then sparkled with excitement.

"I can do it," he said, getting up from the court and bouncing on his feet.

"Yes, you can," replied Chuck as he closed the gate behind him.

Seth played a dynamic set, stunning his opponent with his first serve, making him run from side to side swinging after, but missing, Seth's well-placed shots. Seth was moving well. He was working like never before. The whole team cheered him on. And at the corner of his mouth, you could even detect a smile, a smile he hadn't had in a long time.

Did he win? You'll have to decide, but one thing was for sure: either way he came off the court a happier, more positive person, because, you know, attitude is everything!

Attitudinal Climate

We all choose our own attitude, an "inner climate" that
leads our actions, doings or nondoings for that day, week, or year.
To adjust one's inner climate is a daily task to
find the right balance;
It can be a daily victory if adjusted wisely or a daily defeat
if chosen with haste. When inspiration and motivation encompass
your mind, it feels like warm sun shining on your face
creating smiles and glorious wonder.
We all have a choice (how empowering!) to choose
our inner climate—
our forecast for the day;
So, all truth be told, what would your ideal weather be if you were
giving the forecast in your mind?
We all know people who choose to forecast rain, hail, and
thunderstorms on a daily basis.
We also know people who choose sunshine to warm themselves
and others around them.
Just remember that you choose your inner-weather,
your "attitudinal climate"
So choose wisely and with care—
Choose to forecast sunshine,warmth, and blue skies daily . . .
choose happiness.

© Jami Lynn Bauer

Having a bad attitude will dig you a hole you can't get out of; but having a good attitude will raise you to great heights.
—Megan Lodell, junior high student

Your attitude determines your actions.
—Christy McConkey, junior high student

You have to accept what comes and the only important thing is that you meet it with the best you have to give.
—Elenor Roosevent

My thoughts on attitude

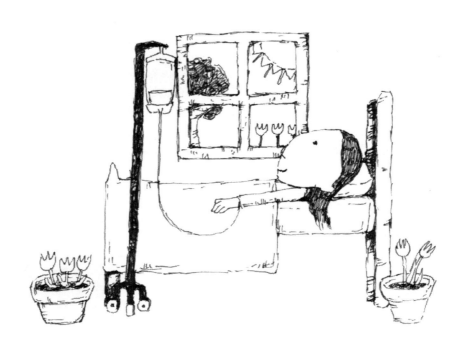

BE GRATEFUL JUST TO PLAY

GRATITUDE

8

GRATITUDE

Be grateful just to play

To be grateful is to appreciate the opportunity just to play. Those who look from side to side to compare themselves with others, let victory and defeat cloud their judgment, or take for granted their opportunity to play are the first to fall when the going gets tough. Having the tools and skills to play is a gift from God. Enjoy this gift as someday it may be taken away from you. Christopher Reeves, better known as Superman, was an icon of television. After being thrown from a horse, he lost the use of his body. Though crippled for life, Reeves provides each one of us with an example of what it means to be grateful just to be alive.

P eggy, you were great today!" said her mother, Suzanne, while helping her carry her swim gear to the car. "I'm so glad I came to watch you swim. It's so much fun to watch you glide through that water. And did you know that you shaved a half of a second off your time in the breast stroke today? We've only been in Colorado Springs for two weeks now and you're already making progress."

Peggy shrugged her shoulders. "Yeah, but I thought I'd beat my time by at least one full second by now. A half, are you sure it's just a half?"

"Peggy!" her mother gave her a disapproving glance, "How can you say that? Be glad about the progress you've made. Coach White says you're doing well, being so new on the team and all."

Peggy sighed. "But Meg and most of the others are swimming faster than me. So it doesn't matter what Coach says. I need to be better now or I'll never make the trials."

"Of course the other girls are faster—they've been on the U.S. team much longer than you. You're younger than them. But you'll catch up. For now think of it as an opportunity to be with the best in the world. Be grateful for the gifts God has given you." Peggy's mother looked her in the eyes. "You know you are one in a million." Peggy said nothing.

She entered her first swim meet at age four. In her first race ever, she placed third and that was after stopping to clear her goggles. At age fourteen, after winning all the freestyle and fly meets she entered, she had long hoped, and even expected, to be interviewed and recruited for the U.S. Olympic team. So to Peggy it was no surprise and no big deal when she was finally invited to train with the team in Colorado Springs during her senior year in high school.

Like every afternoon since their arrival, Peggy's mom, Suzanne, was in high spirits. "Look at those mountains," she said while driving home. Then looking over at her daughter, Suzanne asked, "Peggy, aren't you glad that we can live in such a pretty place?"

Peggy glanced up briefly. "Sure. But I'm in the pool most of the day. How am I to notice?"

When they pulled up to their home, Peggy, without hesitation, hurried to her bedroom and began listing in her tattered notebook everything she had to work on. "(34) Start is slow, (35) Timing is off, (36) Kick is sloppy."

Suzanne carried Peggy's duffel bag into her room and then looked over Peggy's shoulder, noticing her daughter's growing list of personal complaints. Two weeks in Colorado Springs and things were still the same. She sat next to her daughter, glancing at her list. "Peggy, what am I going to do with you? Why can't you see all the good things that are happening to you?" Peggy could only stare at her mother in frustration.

October third began as a routine day for Peggy. She woke up at 5:00 AM to arrive at practice by 5:30. As always, she rounded the corner by the training facility at around 5:20 on her favorite possession, a full-suspension mountain bike that her parents bought her as a gift just after moving to Colorado. Intent on beating her last time, she cut across a lawn, but her tire slipped on the wet grass. She was thrown violently from the bike and landed on the sidewalk. Two passersby quickly phoned the police, and in minutes, Peggy's unconscious body was carried by ambulance to the hospital.

After hours of tests and MRI scans, the doctors met first with Peggy's mom and then with her coaches to tell them that Peggy was in a coma and had broken five bone, including a slight fracture in the cervical area of her spine. Although they thought that she had received no brain damage, because of her helmet, they couldn't be sure.

After more than forty-eight hours without any movement, family, friends, and coaches began to worry about her. Although the life-support machines showed very strong signals, the doctors were not sure if those signals would ever translate into a conscious young girl again. Peggy's mom, coaches, and all others who came to the hospital, decided to pray together, hoping that maybe higher powers could do something for them. Each of them stood in a circle around Peggy's bed. Peggy's mom prayed, and then the group stood in silence.

Meanwhile, Peggy could faintly hear her mother's voice, calling for her to return. She felt like she was somewhere else, fading away from the room into light and peace, into freedom where there was no pain. It was almost like she was watching herself from the corner of the room. Peggy watched the scene from afar and tried to block out her mother's call to come back, but in her state of perfect harmony, she knew that her mother and friends needed her. She knew her life was not supposed to end like this.

Five minutes later, Coach White noticed Peggy's right hand begin to move and her eyes begin to flutter. They called for the doctor as Peggy struggled to come out of her deep and dark sleep. When her eyes opened, she saw her mother, who was sobbing with happiness. Peggy had no real understanding of what had happened to her. She just knew that she was in immense pain and that friends and family were nearby.

As Peggy scanned her covered torso, wrapped in casts and bandages, she closed her eyes to the sight. Her head started to race. "Oh my gosh, what's happened to me? What's wrong with me? What have I done?"

Dr. Lobel, one of the team's physicians, was a resident at the hospital. When Peggy awoke, the doctor was shining a small flashlight in her eyes. "How you doin' Ace?" Ace was his pet name for her. Just his presence helped comfort Peggy, as she had seen him work with other teammates. Peggy began to relax.

"Not so good, Doc. I think I messed myself up pretty bad."

"Well Peg, your body has been through a lot, that's for sure." Dr. Lobel went on to tell her in detail about her broken bones, but left the cuts, bruises, and other minor issues alone. After much time trying to figure out what exactly happened to her, everyone was just happy to see her alive. The overall feelings in the room were undeniably special and loving. It was a natural high of sorts, the kind of feeling that comes over you when you know everything is going to be all right and that you are protected from any harm. Peggy soaked it in. She had never felt this way before.

After watching everyone bask in their sense of love and appreciation for one another, Dr. Lobel finally said to Peggy, "I have to tell you straight, my dear, you may be taking quite a long break from your swimming and it may not be the same for you if and when you return." Peggy lay there in silence.

Peggy lay awake, staring at the white ceiling for hours after her visitors had all left, thinking about her doctor's words. All she could think about was the doctor's voice saying, "It may not be the same for you . . ." She cried aloud and wrestled with desperate feelings. She then remembered her mother's prayer, calling out to her with longing and need. She knew then and there that her life had a greater meaning and purpose. Then she realized she had a choice to see the glass as half-empty or half-full. She then pictured her mother's face just as she saw it floating above her body in the examination room where she lay unconscious. She remembered the feelings of bliss, but even greater, the feelings of belonging to her family and friends. With this image firmly in her mind, Peggy began to recognize all that she had to be grateful for. She had her family. She had her life, the greatest gift anybody could have. She had her experiences of sorrow and grief, humor and love, laughter and anger, pleasure and pain to give her life distinction. She had her body, which, although broken, injured, and bruised, could perhaps be strong again someday.

In the long days that followed, Peggy fell in love with her ability to breathe, eat, drink, see, and make choices, even though she lay in a hospital bed, unable to move as her body tried to heal itself. Everyone around her was amazed at her attitude and at the gratitude she displayed for everything she had been given and those people who cared about her.

Weeks later, Peggy's mom came once again for her daily visit. After some time in the conversation, she looked over at her daughter lying next to her and asked. "Isn't just lying here driving you nuts?"

"Not when you're next to me," said Peg. Her mother smiled. "Plus, I've got lots of new books to read, and CDs to listen to. The team sent them over. You know, they are great."

Several weeks rolled by, and the change in Peggy was evident as she began her rehabilitation exercises. Although tremendously painful, Peggy would clench her teeth and mutter to herself, "Recovery equals work." Despite the pain, Peggy remained grateful for her ability to move her body.

More weeks later, Peggy lay in the hospital bed, clenching her hands together over and over and pulling at the white sheets trying to get comfortable. "Shouldn't Doc Lobel be here by now, Mom?" asked Peggy. Right then Dr. Lobel breezed through the door and sat next to his patient.

"Sorry, I'm late," he said. "I'll get right to what you've been waiting to hear—the news about your condition, progress, future steps of recovery, and," Doc paused, "your release from the hospital."

"Yesss!"

Dr. Lobel smiled and continued, "We're very optimistic about your long-term health and recovery, Peggy. But given the breaks in your pelvis and fractures in your lumbar vertebra we don't know if you'll be able to match your same stroke, same times, you know. We may eventually have to operate and fuse your spine, which took most of the force from your accident. As for the damage to your arms and legs, you're well on your road to recovery. In fact, although we're restricting you to minimal physical activity, you can get in the pool again this week to start rehabilitating and strengthening your muscles."

At this point Peggy was crying uncontrollably. Peggy's mother felt her heart start to ache in her chest for her daughter. She didn't know what to say about the dissolution of Peggy's dreams and hopes.

"Peggy . . ." she began, trying to search for words to calm her daughter's grief.

But Peggy interrupted her mother, smiling joyfully as the tears continued to splatter down her face.

"Mom," she said, "I'm going to be all right. Everything is going to be all right. I just know it." Suzanne gathered her daughter into her arms and knew that Peggy would do what she could to become a champion once again. Olympian or not, she would be grateful just to try.

Simple Pleasures

A whole day goes by and the next
is on its way . . .
what did you do and learn today?
Did you learn to laugh
when your job was too much to bear?
Did you learn to compliment someone,
or just show that you care?
Did you stop to feel love
in a world so full of hate;
Did you learn from a friend, a child, or mate?
The fact is we are learning so much each day
It's like an ongoing course
with no credits or costs . . .
The truth is we must learn each day
or else we'll be lost.

Love,
Still Learning

© Jami Lynn Bauer

Without gratitude you'll never appreciate your sport of your life!
—Kyle Spinder, age 14

Don't let other people be your looking glass.
—Cole D. Hooley, age 18

Gratitude is a fruit of great cultivation; you do not find it among gross people.
—Samuel Johnson (1709–1784)

My thoughts on gratitude

IN THE END IT'S THE
ONLY WAY TO GO

HONESTY

9

HONESTY

In the end it's the only way to go

Honesty is definately the best policy. Just look at those people you know who don't tell the truth. Are they at peace with their lives? Do they seem happy? There is a price to pay for being dishonest and it is never worth the grief. While telling the truth may be the harder of the two choices up front, your peace of mind will benefit you throughout your life. Begin by being honest with yourself. Then, seek to deceive no one, for in the end, you will only be deceiving yourself!

It was the night before their last final exam. Chad and Hunter Williams had been quizzing each other by going over their notes and outlines to make sure they had covered all of their bases. Hunter had decided to call it quits and relax by watching a late-night movie when the phone rang.

"How's it going?" Hunter said, clenching the receiver between cheek and shoulder.

"Hey, Hunter. It's Cal. Loads of parties are developing on frat row tonight. Grab your brother and head on down. Ours is sponsoring one of the biggest fiestas of the year, probably the best party of your entire college career. It'll be a riot."

"I don't know. Chad and I have a monster final tomorrow."

"You've got to come. What time's your exam?"

"3:00 PM."

"No sweat, then. You've got all day! You guys can sack out at my place and leave in the morning."

"Let me talk to my brother." Hunter turned to his brother and filled him in on the party details.

"I don't know, Hunter," said Chad, "West Hamshire is more than two hours away. Let's just get some sleep so we can knock Dr. Eastley's exam out of the park. After all this work, I want to end on a good note. Do you realize that our whole grade is riding on this final? If we don't ace this thing, we could flunk this class—we may not even not graduate!"

"Oh, come on, Chad," Hunter said as he began throwing stuff in a duffel bag. "Let's do it. This is our senior year! A fun night out would be good for us after all of our hard work. I'll even drive—both ways!"

Chad paced around the room a bit, then relented. "All right, all right. But we have to leave by 10:00 AM to get back in time for the exam. After all, it's not the first time we've taken the night off. So far, I've never regretted it." Hunter winked at his brother.

For all of their twenty-two years, the twins had been best friends. Their father, Martin Williams, was an engineer by trade and a part-time professor at an elite private university in Connecticut. Their mother, Vera, taught science at a local high school and was known for her crazy experiments and bizarre sense of humor. The kids loved her. It was an interesting household. When growing up, both Hunter and Chad were given the freedom to do whatever they wanted.

Their parents were so involved with their work that neither spent much time really counseling the children as to what was right and wrong, good and bad, appropriate and inappropriate, honest or dishonest. Both Hunter and Chad were excellent students and their parents thought that if their kids were smart enough to lead their classes academically, then they were certainly smart enough to make good personal decisions. But this wasn't necessarily the case.

When the boys were teenagers, they were very good at deceptive games. They often thrilled their friends with clever stories of deception and trickery. One particular time during lunch, they drove out to the country and purchased twelve piglets, packed them into the back of Calvin's old Land Cruiser, and herded them into the science laboratory. Of course, when Mrs. Andersen entered the facility and screamed at the sight of the wild animals running around the room, everyone had a great laugh.

Rather than being thrown into detention or expelled, Chad and Hunter created a story that nearly landed them extra credit points, making a case for an experiment that could possibly revolutionize the farming industry. No one quite understood the connection, but their story sounded good to all who listened, and the principal gave them the benefit of the doubt. Given that both boys were exceptional students, especially in math and science like their parents, their antics were often ignored by their teachers. Both were also exceptional baseball players, but after one of their teammates almost got hurt by one of their little stunts, both Chad and Hunter were banned from high school sports. Lesson learned? Not yet.

When it was time for college, Chad and Hunter planned to hunker down, organize themselves, and dismiss any risky actions that might jeopardize their scholarships. Along with that came disciplined work and even some respect for their teachers. During their first two semesters, Chad and Hunter showed early promise, and both were invited to be members of a prestigious research team headed by Dr. Eastley. But this was New York City—the city that never sleeps—it was all too tempting.

Upon reaching their third semester, the discipline they had promised one another was exchanged for nights on the town and weekend trips to different schools. This was the college experience they had dreamed of. Several times their colleagues questioned them about their tardiness and slipping grades because if affected them as well. Each time, both Chad and Hunter created some crazy excuse just to get by. Most of the time their teachers and classmates believed their stories, and sometimes they just wrote it off to two smart kids having a good time. Anyway, by the time senior year came around, both boys had done enough work earn them degrees. The only thing left was Dr. Easley's upper-level chemistry class.

Of course, as with all the other parties and weekend trips, this particular night out was a smash hit—lots of people, girls, food, dancing, and late-night Chinese. Morning came mighty fast, and although the sun shone brightly through the window of Calvin's living room, neither the sun nor the noise from the street below could wake the group.

Around 2:00 PM, Hunter raised his eyelids and searched for the nearest clock. Seeing the red digital lights flash 12:00 AM . . . 12:00 AM . . . 12:00 AM, he quickly realized that somebody must have knocked the plug out of the wall socket. Peering at yet another clock, this time a battery powered one, he jumped up in shock.

"Chad!" he yelled, grabbing for his clothes and the car keys. Chad was equally frightened. After gathering their stuff from around the apartment, the two jumped in the car and sped off for their final.

Unfortunately, sixty miles into their drive, they came across a state patrolman, who wrote them up for driving eighty-five. What did it matter now. They were late anyway.

During the rest of their drive home, the boys put their heads together and managed to develop a story that would hopefully convince Dr. Eastley of their unfortunate circumstances. They drove straight to their professor's classroom, arriving around 4:45 PM—right in the middle of the exam. They requested his presence in the hallway so they could quietly tell him their story. Dr. Eastley was terribly curious and wondered how their story might compare with the others that they had concocted throughout their college careers.

"So, you see, sir, we did go to the party in West Hamshire and maybe we shouldn't have," Hunter admitted. "But as we were leaving, we noticed one of our tires had been slashed. Is that a bummer or what?"

Then Chad chimed in. "We looked all over for a tire store that carried the right size of tires," Chad said. But we couldn't find a place until noon. Good thing we had enough cash to pay the bill."

"We're so sorry, sir," Hunter said, looking out the window. "But we studied hard for this exam. We're ready, and we'd like to take it."

Dr. Eastley folded his arms and thought for a minute.

"Okay, gentlemen," he finally said. "Go home, clean up, and return at 7:00 PM for a special sitting of the exam." The boys were elated.

"Thanks so much, Dr. Eastley," said Hunter and Chad. They shook their professor's hand and left his office, clearing the sweat from their brows. As they walked out of the building, they looked at each another and sighed with relief.

"That was a beauty, Chad." Hunter grinned at his brother. "And so simple too."

"Yep, we just averted a most certain disaster.. Too bad we had to make up such elaborate stories in the past. The simple ones seem to work the best."

At 6:45 PM, after cleaning up and quickly reviewing their notes, the brothers arrived at Dr. Eastley's office to take their final exam of their college careers.

"Chad . . . Hunter," Dr. Eastley greeted them. "Take your pens and pencils, grab your calculators and go into rooms 128 and 130 across the hall from each other." The two boys headed off to their respective rooms.

"You have two hours to complete the exam. Remember, this is worth seventy-five percent of your grade. Good luck, gentlemen."

At the one-and-a-half-hour mark, both brothers were well into the last set of questions, each feeling comfortable with his answers and each hoping the other was having the same good luck. But in this case, luck was not on their side.

As each of them got to the last of their exam they were shocked by what they saw. As both Hunter and Chad stared in disbelief, wondering what the other might say, a sick feeling came over them. The last question read, "For 90 percent of your grade, which of your tires was slashed?" In their own rooms, in their own silence, each was stunned. They had only a 25 percent chance of graduating!

"Honest Lies"

You look at me and I can see that something passed me by;
I look back at you and it's just an "honest lie."
To tell the truth, oh, it's not a sin,
for when you lie you never win;
It's yourself that loses and your soul feels pain,
so tell the truth—what's there to gain?
Your honest lies hurt more than heal,
look at yourself—now how do you feel?
Can you feel comfortable telling these honest lies?
Do they serve a purpose, these lies you tell;
does it make you feel good—do you ever feel well?
I can't understand what there is there to gain,
The only emotion you should feel is shame.
It's your own self worth you put on the line,
so you be the judge . . . do you think it's just fine?
Think it through first, then show no disguise,
rise above all the rest and avoid "honest lies."

© Jami Lynn Bauer

Be honest with everyone, most of all yourself.
—Jenny Linton, junior high student

It's a tougher road to take. But in the long run honesty is worth it.
—Cassie Rhodes, junior high student

Whatsoever things are true, whatsoever things are honest, whatsoever things are just, whatsoever things are pure, whatsoever things are lovely, whatsoever things are of good report; if there be any virtue, and if there be any praise, think on these things.
—2 Corinthians 4:8

My thoughts on honesty

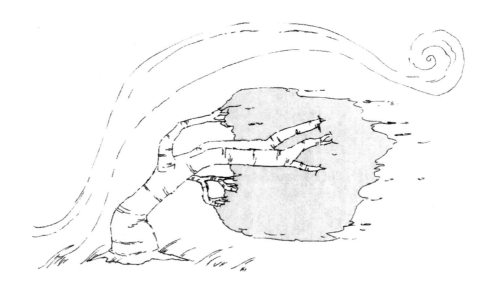

ANYTHING TOO STIFF WILL
SURELY BREAK

FLEXIBILITY

10

FLEXIBILITY

Anything too stiff will surely break

While many do not believe that flexibility is as important as other qualities, it is, in fact, critical for anyone who wishes to succeed in the longterm. Flexibility is a natural quality. It's just as important for the willow tree as it is for the human being. The storms of life will surely come, but those who remain flexible will withstand the wind, the rain, and the hail while the others will fall. Developing this quality will serve you well when the storms of life are on the horizon.

It was a rainy evening with a howling wind. Everyone had gone to bed except for Brittany and her teddy bear. Like always, she was up until late in the night studying for her favorite classes, chemistry and physics, by the soft yellow light in the living room. As the weather outside continued to wreak havoc on the neighborhood, Brittany stared out the front window in awe of the power of nature. She also looked out to check on her favorite tree, a mighty oak that barely moved in the powerful winds.

In many ways, Brittany's father was like this tree, a big and strong man, standing six-foot-five-inches tall. He was a hero to Brittany and the rest of the family. A successful stockbroker on Wall Street, a leader in the community, a dedicated father, and a mentor to many of the young boys in the neighborhood; Stu was seen by many as the quintessential success story. His only weakness seemed to be his lack of flexibility. He was a moster of order and rules. Everything he did had to be planned out and executed with the utmost precision. His job, his leadership roles, even his time with his family fell under strict guidelines.

Just as with his staff at his Wall Street office, Mr. Johns was very strict with the way he ran his family. Awake at dawn, to bed by 10:00pm; meals, chores, and all other duties were planned. Brittany's father was what many people call a Type A personality, the kind of person who is driven and outgoing, pushing himself to the limit to be the best in everything that he did. And it showed.

Brittany was much like her father. Her life was scheduled, and school work always came first. She was a straight-A student without a blemish on her record. She was well dressed, well groomed, and well mannered. In fact, Brittany was so structured and driven like her father that many of her friends called her "the machine" with reference to her ability to crank out late nights, big projects, and top quality work—usually at the expense of a social life. These were the qualities that Brittany loved and appreciated about her father, and one of her greatest goals was to be just like him.

Like everything else, if things didn't go as planned at home or at the office, Stu was frustrated. For a long time, Stu's doctor had warned him about his difficulty handling stress and change.

For years Stu kept up with his routines and strict discipline until one hot August night when the worst happened. Stu had a massive heart attack and died before anybody could save him. Upon speaking with the doctors, it was obvious why Stu died so young—stress and overwork. When all was said and done, what Stu Johns left behind were his beliefs and principles about the world, his life, and his work ethic.

Mr. Johns' death was a shock to everybody, especially Brittany. She took it harder than anyone else. She was so close to him, never wanting to leave his side whenever he was home. She watched him, copied him, and did everything to please him. She ignored all of his faults and focused on the many great qualities he displayed, trying to be like him in every way possible, especially in the way she tackled her school work.

Brittany got along wonderfully with teachers at school—with most of them at least. But there was this one teacher, Dr. Ellsworth, that Brittany wasn't quite sure of. Dr. Ellsworth taught World Religions, an advanced class that covered the basics of the world's religious history. His lackadaisical nature and often unstructured ways of teaching led her to believe that he was somewhat of a goof. In fact, Dr. Ellsworth's approach, unlike other teachers, actually allowed each student to choose his or her own criteria for being graded. This left Brittany dumbfounded and angry, and she let Dr. Ellsworth know it.

One day after class, Brittany stayed to talk to her teacher about his manner of teaching. Dr. Ellsworth was waiting for this day to come. He had been watching Brittany over a long period of time and knew she came from a family of overachievers. He knew of her father's death and saw that Brittany was on her way to early burnout herself. So he thought it was important that Brittany learn to be a little more flexible in her thinking. Given their different points of view, it was only a matter of time before a confrontation would occur. The day had come.

"Dr. Ellsworth, can I talk to you for a moment?"

"Sure Brittany, what can I do for you?"

"To tell you the truth, I'm a little confused about what we are doing in class. I mean, in every other class I'm given outlines, chapters to read, and a framework for getting my assignments done. There are problems to solve and questions to answer. There are right answers and there are wrong answers. What I'm trying to say is, what's up with religion! I mean of all the classes, I thought the big man upstairs would be pretty straight forward. You know, follow the commandments and all that type of stuff. But look at us, everybody has a different point of view. We're all graded differently. There are no answers. Help me out here, please!"

"Brittany. What's your favorite subject?"

"Anything related to the hard sciences, I guess. Why?"

"And why is that?"

"Because I can make sense of the information. Because there are specific answers to questions and because there is reason behind the logic. Things are testable, repeatable, consistent."

"But haven't you noticed that over time our knowledge changes, even in the hard sciences? I mean look at Newton and Galileo. Didn't they change the way we look at the world? And what about Einstein's theory of relativity? Who would think that time and space were connected? How do you explain those changes?"

"Yes, so things have changed. We've learned, though. We are smarter now than we ever have been. The answers exist."

"Well, what about God, then?"

"What about God?"

"So you believe there is a God?" said Dr. Ellsworth.

"Of course there is a God ."

"Well, is God male? Is there only one of them?"

"Of course those things are true. Everybody, including you, should know that!"

"And who taught you all that you know about God?"

"My mother and father," said Brittany.

"So what about the rest of the world. Some believe in one God, but others believe in numerous gods. Some worship idols, ancestors, and even trees and plants. What are you going to say to them?"

"What's your point, Dr. Ellsworth."

"The point is that there are many different perspectives in life, many different approaches on how to do things, what to believe, and what to put your trust in. The fact that somebody does something differently than you think is right is no reason to brush them off. The fact is, we don't know who is right and who is wrong. What we do know is that there is a whole world of beliefs out there and many ways of learning, knowing, and experiencing the world. Some of us like books, others like to observe the world, and others like to experiment by doing things. Some need structure, some only need support and a few books. My class is about finding who you are and what your style is. And it looks like you are finding that out for yourself now. How do you feel about that?"

At this point Brittany began to get Dr. Ellsworth's point. She understood that her classmates were different from her, but she didn't like it. She wanted everybody to conform to the way she did things. So much diversity was frustrating for her.

"I guess I'm a little angry at the whole thing," she replied. "I always wished that life was just a set of formulas and all you had to do was figure out the problems. I don't like the fact that there are a million answers out there and no one really knows which one is right."

"Maybe they are all right in their own way," replied Dr. Ellsworth.

"That could be, but that makes everything so difficult. Look at my father. He was a great man and knew what he believed. He did things in a very calculated and organized way, and he was successful. I thought that everyone, including me, should be just like him. He taught me everything that I know."

"But look at what happened Brittany…"

For a moment Brittany looked stunned. It never really occurred to her that her father's philosophy of life might have been part of the reason behind his early death. Brittany's eyes became misty.

"It's just not fair," Brittany yelled as she began weeping on Dr. Ellsworth's shoulder. As the tears began to fall, Dr. Ellsworth consoled her as best he could.

When her tears began to quiet some ten minutes later, she felt a huge burden lift from her shoulders. For the first time she realized what she had become: a robot like her father. It was the first time anybody had helped her see that her behavior was leading her down a path of self-destruction. When she thought about this, Brittany came to realize that there might be a better way to live her life. For the first time in years, she was open to suggestions.

"So what do you think I should do, Dr. Ellsworth?"

"Have you ever tried getting a C grade before?"

"No!" Brittany yelled emphatically. "You have got to be kidding!"

"No I'm not. When was the last time you went with your friends to a movie, went out on a date, rode your bike in the woods, walked nowhere in particular, sat for an hour and thought about nothing, cooked a meal you have never cooked before, threw rocks into a stream?"

"I don't remember. I'm usually home studying. In fact, now that I think about it, that's all I do."

"Exactly what I mean. You should start going out and doing something different, out of the blue, and a bit crazy. You know, start having a little fun once in a while."

"Maybe you are right. Maybe I could lighten up a little bit and try something new and different. Maybe I will hit the movies this week and take a few hours off from my studies. I have a perfect GPA, but no friends to share my life with. It's time to change that, huh?" For a while, neither Dr. Ellsworth nor Brittany said anything. They both just took in the moment. Brittany then turned to Dr. Ellsworth and thanked him for spending the time with her.

Just twenty minutes earlier, Brittany had a major problem with her teacher, and now somehow he was a new mentor to her, second to her dad of course. She had totally forgotten why she was there in the first place, and it didn't seem to matter, because now she saw things a little differently.

Many thoughts began to roll around in her head, and rather than take the bus, Brittany decided to do something a little different and walk home. This would give her time to think over all that she had heard.

Before leaving the building, Brittany stopped at the gym and watched the women's gymnastics team practicing their routines. One of the girls in her science class, Tess, who was stocky and not very limber, attempted a back hand spring and winced in pain as she pulled both of her leg muscles. She had forgotten to stretch.

On her way home, Brittany came across another scene that intrigued her. As she was walking down Main Street, she passed a local karate studio where yoga was being taught. She could see through the front window that a class was in session. She was amazed what those girls could do. Some were thin, others were heavy, but all were more flexible than anybody she had ever seen before.

Brittany then began thinking about what she and Dr. Ellsworth had been talking about, this whole idea of seeing things from a different perspective and becoming flexible in one's approach to life. Realizing that she was always walking down the same streets, Brittany decided to find another street that led her to her house. She was equally amazed by how many new things were there, things that she had never seen before. There were new stores, new trees, even a small pond that she had never known existed. Rather than walk, Brittany began to jog. She had never done that. She took in all the new scenery and enjoyed every minute of it. It was a new world to her. Little did she know that this new world had always existed. She just had never chosen a different path.

When Brittany got home, her mother asked when she would like her regular Monday night meal, a big salad and a grilled cheese sandwich. She replied that anything she wanted to make was fine with her. Her mother was blown away. After watching TV for an hour, Brittany's mother came in and asked if she was all right, as this was one of the only times her mother had seen her watch anything that wasn't "educational." Brittany assured her mother that everything was all right and that she had had one of the best days of her life.

After her macaroni and cheese dinner—another first—Brittany decided that doing at least some homework was probably a good thing, as she still didn't agree with the C grade idea. As she unpacked her bag, she could hear the wind pick up outside. Everyone was in bed, and once again she was alone. Within minutes, lightening was cracking and hard rain was pelting the house. Brittany grabbed her bag and went right to her favorite chair in front of the living room window so she could see her favorite tree. Like many nights, the rain was hard, but particularly strong were the gusts of wind. Brittany stared at the mighty oak for a minute and then jumped right in to her opened religion text. Tonight she would begin somewhere in the middle of the book.

Brittany dug deeply into her studies of Taoism and Buddhism and was amazed by the different outlooks people around the world had. Suddenly she heard a loud cracking sound. Brittany looked outside, only to see her favorite tree standing straight and tall, moving for no earthly forces, while the limber willows swayed violently in the direction of the wind. As she looked more closely, she could see the bark flying off the mighty oak, and within seconds the oak began to move. As she looked at the base of the tree, Brittany could see large branches breaking from the power of the wind. Suddenly the tree was at the mercy of the wind, which took its toll.

Feeling insecure and frightened, Brittany couldn't believe her eyes. The mighty oak was breaking, losing limbs, and being utterly destroyed by the elements, while the willows were left standing, waving to and fro with all the flexibility and resiliency of the yoga students she had seen just hours before.

The tree that had comforted her for the bulk of her life was coming apart, just like her dad. Brittany didn't know how to feel, but she wanted to remain alone. As she kept looking at the damaged tree, she noticed something that had never really captured her attention before. It was those willow trees. They were still standing despite all of the wind and rain.

As she continued to ponder, she felt that no conversation could have been so timely as the one she just had with Dr. Ellsworth that day.

Detours of Life

I drive ahead, going straight towards my goals,
my path appears clear and I feel in control.
Ahead in the distance I encounter an
unplanned design,
It looks like a stranger's pathway—
although I know it's mine;
Envisioning smooth roads in the "highway of life"
what pleasant thoughts to possess . . .
are the roads ever that nice?
They're not always smooth, nor free of construction;
we must come to realize this to avoid self-destruction;
For there are often times roadblocks, yield signs,
and other deviations we can not avoid—
They challenge our souls, these "detours of life";
They may seem like a burden,
these roadblocks we must face;
Nevertheless, everything under construction
is done for a purpose to repair and make better.
Drive through the detours and realize your roadblocks.
Keep moving forward to your life's destination
You'll soon see that those setbacks will help you suffice—
for they are only temporary roadblocks
in the highway of life.

© Jami Lynn Bauer

I try to keep both my body and my mind flexible. That way, when the tough times come, I'm ready for them.
—Melissa Zotell, ninth grade

If you are not flexible, you can snap!
—Andreana Clegg, ninth grade

I never pre-determine my game. It's always creative.
—Michael Jordan

My thoughts on flexibility

KEEP EVERYTHING
IN PERSPECTIVE
HUMOR

11

HUMOR

Keep everything in perspective

Without humor what's the fun of life? While there is so much to do and accomplish in this life, make sure to have some fun. Many people who strive for great success get lost in the goal and forget the great joy that comes with being in the game. Many refuse to enjoy themselves for fear that they won't be their best. The secret is, without fun you can never become your best, because over time, if you do not enjoy what you do, you'll never stick out through the tough times. Try having fun each day of your life—both in and out of your sporting arena. You might even find that a little humor will take you a long way on your road to high performance.

Spring had finally sprung and it was time for optimism and fun on the soccer field. But so far playing soccer for the JFK women's team hadn't been much fun at all. The JFK bulldogs had been a losing team for three years in a row, and this year Coach Donovan made up her mind to get serious about her team. She was a tough coach, but that wasn't working. Now was the time to really step up the intensity. That meant sprints, drills, late afternoon practices, and even more discipline. Sweepers and fullbacks were no longer allowed their occasional shots at goal. Each girl was to play her position and stick to the book on technique and strategy.

With the new code of conduct in place, the team did see some improvement: four wins and just three losses—a huge improvment over last year. There seemed to be only one problem: nobody was having much fun. Tension filled the air, and small, ridiculous arguments began to emerge at practices and games. Frustrations ran high and today was no different.

The game was in the third quarter, and JFK was down 1 to 2 against last year's conference champions. Every girl seemed to be playing her position well, yet something wasn't working. Angie, frustrated and exhausted, had made twelve attempts at a goal with no success. Coach Donovan pulled her off the field to give her a rest.

"Good work," Coach said as she handed Angie a water bottle. "Let's sink a few of those shots out there, okay?"

Angie, like the other girls on the sidelines, looked unusually frustrated. "I don't know why they're not going in Coach. I'm just so tense."

"Tense, why are you tense?"

"I don't know. I'm working so hard out there. Maybe I'm trying too hard—like the rest of the girls. I mean just look at them."

As Coach Donovan peered out onto the field, she could see obvious signs of stress. Nobody was in their flow. Their tight, jerky motions, combined with angry faces, didn't look like the team she envisioned.

"We're winning more than last year, but this isn't right," Coach Donovan said to herself. Angie splashed the rest of the water on her face and neck. "Can I go back in now, Coach?" she asked, bouncing on the balls of her feet.

"Rest up. You'll be back in, in a few minutes."

After her conversation with Coach Donovan, Angie sat on the wood bench only to find Reggie, her boyfriend of two months, stopping by after band practice to watch the game. Reggie was famous at JFK High for three things: loud, obnoxious guitar solos; his hair style (or lack therof); and his rather charming wit. He made everyone laugh, including his teachers, which was why Angie, a clean-cut halfback with a nervous father, liked him so much. He was different.

One look at Angie's face and Reggie knew there was something wrong. "What up, Angie? Looks like you're gonna get sick, cry . . . something."

"You're very perceptive!"

"Your taking this soccer thing much too seriously again. Aren't you?"

With a stern look, Angie turned to her soon-to-be ex-boyfriend. "Of course I'm taking it seriously. How am I supposed to improve, get noticed, even recruited if I don't give one hundred percent all the time?"

"If you think missing a dozen shots on goal will get you noticed, you're right; but it's not the kind you are looking for. Sounds like that trying harder stuff isn't working."

Angie peered at him.

"Okay, okay. This conversation obviously isn't working. Let's look at this a little differently." Quickly Reggie grabbed Angie's hand and pulled her down on the grass next to him. "I've got another idea: how about having some fun out there. I mean, what's this all for anyway? Do you like kicking that ball around or is this some kind of personal mission?" Angie softly answered, "I don't know. Seems like I've spent so much time trying to impress Coach and turn this team around that I kind of forgot about the fun part."

"Hey, Angie, you've got one minute left. Let's get ready!" hollered Coach Donovan.

Seeing an opportunity, Reggie grabbed hold of his girlfriend and whispered something into her ear. At that moment Angie's eyes began to twinkle while her mouth gave way to a bellowing throng of laughter. Some of the girls looked over from the sidelines while others were looking over from across the field. Seeing their captain loosen up a little, some even cracked smiles themselves.

"Come on, Angie. Get in there" yelled Coach Donovan, glaring at young Reggie as if he was an intruder in her den of influence.

"Coming, Coach." Angie jumped back in the game. Reggie, sitting all by himself, was grinning from ear to ear, looking as if he'd just sucked in six helium balloons. Putting on his floppy leather hat and readying himself to wreak havoc somewhere else, Reggie looked in Mrs. Donovan's direction and shouted at the top of his voice, "Hey JFK, why don't we have some fun out there today!" Again came the look that most students don't dare to confront—the stinkface. Coach Donovan was known for it.

The next scene was Angie running down the field with the ball. She was out of position but pulling some awesome moves. She emerged from the crowd of jerseys, hurtling to the goal. A quick fake and some fancy footwork later, Angie stuck the ball into the top right corner of the net. Reggie cheered and the team went wild. Angie was amazed at how easy it was. "That was fun," she thought to herself, peering at Reggie, who was at least fifty feet away from Coach Donovan.

With only five minutes remaining, the score was finally tied, three-all. The other team called a time-out, and Reggie began floating around the team's benches, once again carrying on conversations and cracking jokes like only he could. Coach Donovan wasn't happy about this. He was disrupting her team, her structure, and her rules. Although the girls seemed to be having fun, Coach Donovan was quick to shush the young jester. But Reggie kept right on disrupting and the girls seemed to like it. They started to cheer and make noise. This was quite different from the last few games.

There were four minutes left, then three, then two. The score was still tied 3-3. Once again Angie and Rachel, her cocaptain, were in a breakaway, passing the ball back and forth through a sea of opposing colors. As they maneuvered through the pack, Angie, using her left foot, passed the ball to Rachel, giving her a clear shot on goal—which she made with only seconds left in the game. The rest of the team rushed the field in a fit of excitement and carried their two captains off the field. What a game.

Back in the locker room, Coach Donovan gathered the team around for a little postgame talk. After giving her congratulations to the team, Coach Donovan once again reinforced her rough and tough approach to winning: play by the book with brutal efficiency, clear strategy, and textbook maneuvers. The girls' stone cold faces said it all.

"Girls, you've been diligent and have worked hard for the past several weeks. Now, as you can see, your hard work is beginning to pay off. You're beginning to look like the athletes I've trained."

The dissenters came early into the conversation.

"Coach?" Samantha broke in, "If I may also make an observation, I think what happened out there was also a matter of not trying so hard. We were loose. We had a good time. I think that's why we won." Many of the girls nodded their heads.

"It was that Reggie Schmidt. He was the one making us laugh," came a voice from the back of the room. Nobody disagreed with this statement, but Coach looked visibly annoyed as she stared at the girl in the back. Coach Donovan paused for a moment then shrugged her shoulders in surrender. "Who knows? Maybe you're right, but I certainly don't want to lose this team's work ethic to Angie's boyfriend. We have a good thing going here and we'll soon have to prove ourselves to bigger and better teams. . . . Anyway, great game. Now get a good night's rest and I'll see you tomorrow."

As the girls left the locker room, they saw Reggie standing by the exit, scanning the players for Angie. As each girl passed, she thanked him for his support and his part in their winning the game. Reggie, as always, was smiling from ear to ear.

"Hey, Reg, why don't you show up for more games. We could really use you," said Rachel, patting his arm as she passed.

"I may just do that!" Reggie replied, flopping his hat over to the left side of his head.

Days later, Rachel and Angie stayed after Friday practice to help organize the field house. They thought this would be a good way of demonstrating team leadership. After gathering and organizing all the equipment, Coach Donovan offered to take the girls out for a bite to eat. Knowing that Rachel and Angie were two of her team's most respected leaders, she thought this might be a good time to check-in and see how the rest of the team was doing.

In the car and at the restaurant there wasn't much conversation—just a lot of small talk mixed in with long pauses of silence. This was probably because the girls were not always in agreement with their well-intentioned coach. Each struggled for the right words. Finally, at the table Angie felt compelled to break the silence.

"Coach, Donovan," Angie said as she unwrapped her burger, "may I speak freely?"

"Please do," she replied.

"While I respect your focus on discipline, I do believe we should have a little more fun out there," Rachel stopped in the middle of a bite of food and looked up at Coach Donovan. Coach Donovan politely listened but disagreed with her captain.

"I understand your point Angie, but I'm not sure that's the right move. I'm dedicated to making you and the rest of the team the best soccer players you can be. I'm not sure letting everyone run around like wild animals is the way to do that." Angie rolled her eyes.

Then Rachel had a few words of her own to say, joining her friend in releasing the tension. After an hour and a half of conversation, both the girls and Coach Donovan acknowledged one another's views but agreed to disagree. Coach Donovan had her beliefs about how to coach the team and the girls had theirs.

On their way home that evening, Coach Donovan, who was giving Angie and Rachel a ride home, stopped at the intersection of Third and Baker Street, not knowing that an intoxicated freshman from another high school had decided to take a joyride in his father's new BMW. As he took the corner at forty miles an hour, it was too late for the girls to avoid the inevitable. In a split second, a deafening crash pierced the air—the twisted cars sat hissing.

All you could see was spidered glass, crumpled metal, and a ton of steam. Both Angie and Rachel lay in the backseat unconscious and, by the looks of it, badly hurt. Coach Donovan, a true believer in seat belts, sat in shock, feeling a strong burn from the seat belt's lash across her neck.

When both girls awoke, panic gripped them. For a moment they heard nothing except a few stray noises coming from the hood of the car. As this eerie, quiet feeling passed, they could hear a faint noise in the distance as police cars and fire trucks were coming towards them. Rachel began screaming with fright.

"I can't move, I can't move," she repeated in a high, gasping voice. "The car might catch on fire. We have to get out of here!"

Coach Donovan quickly unbuckled herself to check on the two girls, both pinned by the crash board. As she looked at their trapped legs, she began to fear her girls were in great physical danger. In a frenzy, Coach Donovan began peppering questions: "Angie, can you feel your legs? Rachel, are you bleeding? Don't panic, girls. Just don't panic." Coach Donovan's voice got higher and higher as she repeated her questions and looked frantically around the cramped space, pushing with her shaking hands against the bent metal.

Coach Donovan's good intentions were only making things worse, and Rachel began to cry. Angie, although worried and in pain, interrupted the moment. "Coach," she said, "It's okay. Let's all try to quiet down for a minute, relax, and wait for help." Although it took a few moments, Coach Donovan listened, took a deep breath, and began to calm down.

After a few moments of quiet reflection and silence, Angie remembered some of the funny things that Reggie had said to her to cheer her up and change the mood. She decided to share one of these stories with her pale friend sitting next to her. "Hey, Rach, remember the time we were driving to the tournament in Alpine City? You and half of the team were in the van with Reggie and I was following you in the wagon."

"Yea, what about it?" Rachel asked, her voice still shaking.

"Remember how badly we covered your car in food? You could hardly tell the car was silver."

Rachel's sobs soon died down and out of her mouth came a shaky chuckle. "True," she said. "But nothing beat the water balloon that took off your passenger-side mirror."

"You got me there. That mirror cost me fifty bucks! You still owe me!"

Within moments, the spirit inside the car changed, as both Angie and Rachel started reminiscing about other food fights and long road trips during the summer, when soccer was played just for fun. Both girls kept laughing yet winced every time they moved. Coach Donovan didn't know what to think or do. She just sat back and listened.

"Have you ever had a food fight, Coach Donovan?" asked Rachel. Coach Donovan thought for a minute. "Well, when I was younger, I remember throwing spaghetti noodles in my brother's face from across the table. Because my brother was only two, he really didn't have much of a chance of dodging the tomato bomb I hurled at him. I laughed so hard watching him try to remove that mess from his forehead, I practically wet my pant—until, of course, my parents walked in. They didn't think it was that funny. In fact, I was grounded for a week. My parents were quite strict, you know."

"Well, maybe we can bring some spaghetti during our next road trip!" Angie started laughing again.

"I'll think about it," replied a much calmer Coach Donovan.

Several moments later, the emergency vehicles arrived. Coach Donovan again tried to open the door handles while the rescuers peered into the pile of glass and steel. "Hold on ladies, we've got to pry the doors open to get you out. You're going to be okay. Just keep doing what you're doing in there and stay calm."

As the city police and fire department continued to work on the doors, Angie, Rachel, and Coach Donovan kept the air light with conversation—trying to ignore their predicament. It took six men and a "jaws of life" mechanism to remove both girls and Coach Donovan from the wreck.

When the crew finally broke through the twisted wreck, the women were taken to the nearest hospital for examination. Rachel suffered minimal damage: a bruised chest and a fractured big toe. Angie, however, broke her right kneecap and left femur. Coach

Donovan was treated for a mild case of shock, then stayed after her release to be with her girls.

As she left the hospital, Coach Donovan paused in the doorway of Angie's hospital room. "I want to thank you girls for your bravery tonight. I was a wreck, and you changed the entire mood in that car. I was really scared for you girls, but you were the strong ones. Thank you." Later that night everybody was home safe and sound.

By the following Monday, it seemed like everybody had heard the terrible story. During lunch hour, Mr. Reynolds, the principle of the school, was eating at a nearby table with Mr. Delphry. Looking over at the table where most of the girl's soccer team ate, they noticed, instead of a lot of grief, half the team chuckling and laughing about the incident. Little did they know that most of the conversations revolved around the stories told in the car, instead of the injuries sustained by the their two leaders.

On the field at 3:30 PM, sixteen girls came ready to play while Rachel and Angie stayed on the sidelines, one with a protective shoe cast and the other on crutches. Today was a big day for the JFK soccer team. After losing to their rival, Jefferson High, three years in a row, Coach Donovan had something to prove and was intent on coaching her best game.

Angie and Rachel had been replaced by two juniors, Elizabeth and Robin. Right from the start, these two less-experienced players hit the field hard, ready to kick some Jefferson High butt; instead, they overran the ball, took too many risks, and blew every shot on goal.

"Let's do it again!" cried Robin. "We have to try harder this time!" Coach Donovan called a time-out and the girls came off the field. "Coach," said Robin breathlessly. "I want another chance. I can feel the goal coming."

After speaking to all of the girls, Coach Donovan pulled Liz and Robin into a separate huddle. At first Coach Donovan was intent on giving them yet another lecture, but then noticed Angie and Rachel looking on. She had an idea. Instead of coaching by the book, she said: "Girls, what's the funniest experience you've ever had in your life?" She then looked back over to Angie and Rachel and grinned. Listening to hear what Coach was saying to her two new, but temporary stars, Angie and Rachel were overcome with the profound change in their coach. They were proud. The night they had spent in the wrecked car and the hospital wasn't for naught. Instead, it was the beginning of a new coach, a new team.

The next morning the *Sunday Star* read, "JFK Women's Soccer Team 6, Jefferson 3." Below the caption, a picture showed two injured players with their coach. The rest of the team was out of focus. Rumor has it they were all laughing.

Humor Me

What role does laughter play in your day-to-day world?
When you lose your grin you begin to lose
the fun life has to offer.
So when you've had a trying day and it seems
like life has put you on a burner so hot and unbearable,
give yourself a smile and laugh and jump into a cool pool nearby.
This world is a daily challenge and the biggest victory is if
you can laugh at yourself . . .
then share your joy with the world.
Remember this motto and practice it regularly for health,
happiness, and well-being;
"GRINNERS ARE WINNERS . . . SO SMILE A LOT!"

© Jami Lynn Bauer (written with a smile)

Laughter is the best medicine, especially when you are losing.
—Charley Welch, seventh grade

Humor makes life much happier.
—Christi McConkey, junior high student

You grow up the day you have your first real laugh at yourself.
—Ethel Barrymore

My thoughts on humor

A LIFE WITHOUT BALANCE
IS NOT A LIFE AT ALL

BALANCE

12

BALANCE

A life without balance is not a life at all

For those who compete and wish to be their best, finding balance can be a tricky chore. However tough to maintain, balance is one of the keys to finding great success. When one is balanced, one can draw on many sources of energy and comfort. When one isn't balanced, any problem can turn into a life-changing event. Seek to find balance in your life. Don't play too much, read too much, sleep too much, eat too much, or speak too much. You will find in life that everything can be taken too far. Learn to balance the physical, mental, emotional, social, and even spiritual parts of your life. By doing this, you will be gearing yourself up not only for great success, but also for great happiness.

It was 7:45 PM on a Thursday night in August, and Darin and Sam, as always, were waiting on Darin's front porch with cards in hand.

"It's getting pretty chilly out here. Where are the rest of the guys?" said Sam.

"Running late, I guess," replied Darin. The two best friends looked at each other but said nothing further. Both could feel that summer's end had come.

"Can you believe it? Two more weeks and we'll be seniors." Darin looked at Sam in disbelief while Darin's mom peeked around the edge of the door.

"Hi, you two. Is the pack coming over tonight?" she asked.

"Of course," Darin said as he shuffled the cards once more. " . . . just warming up the cards."

"So Sam, how's golf practice going?" Darin's mom asked.

"This guy's awesome, mom," Darin answered before Sam could even open his mouth. "Did you know he kept a two handicap last season? Now he's got all these universities after him. He can do whatever he wants; right, Sammy?"

"Well, I've got a good shot at some pretty good schools. I'll definitely keep you posted, Mrs. Johns."

"I look forward to it, Sam. Oh, there's Harold, I'll go in and fix you boys something for the game tonight. I know there's not too many of these nights left. Let me see what I can whip up. Hello Harold!" Mrs. Johns waved.

"Hello Mrs. Johns," Harold waved back, looking at his watch and noticing that he was about twenty minutes late. This was odd because Harold was always early for the weekly card game; he was probably reading something, the two boys thought.

"How's it going, Harold?" Sam called out.

"Good, good." Harold was smiling. "Got my new physics books today—couldn't put 'em down. Sorry I'm late. Got to be thinking about my AP classes, you know."

"Yea, yea, yea," mumbled both Sam and Darin.

The three of them talked until eight, when Eric finally showed up, just coming from his nightly fourteen-mile run. Eric, another usual on-timer, had his own passion—football! He always came to the game sweaty.

"Hey, how was your run?" chimed the group in almost perfect unison.

"Good," Eric said as he plopped down on the ground to begin his well-rehearsed stretching routine. "I'm getting faster and faster, which should help me convince some of those Division I scouts that I'm the running back for them. Where's Jake?"

"Oh, he'll be late. I saw him with some cute brunette."

"Another one?"

"That guy is too lucky; I hate him."

"Tell that to his face. Here he is," said Darin to Harold.

As expected, Jake arrived nearly an hour late.

"Hello, my brothers," Jake grinned as he pulled up a wicker chair. "You would not believe who I was just with . . . " The howling and laughter began.

Unlike most teenage boys, these guys respected one another for both their similarities and their differences. They shared their dreams and their fears, often during card nights, each confiding in the other. Since this was one of their last games before school, more things than usual were on their minds. It would soon be time to conquer again.

About an hour into a strikingly boring game of poker, the conversation began focusing on Eric and his all-state aspirations; next, Sam and his goal of playing golf for Stanford the following fall; and then Harold and his desire to attend Cal Tech. Jake also had his personal goals—becoming a successful model and dating the most popular girl in school, Becky. Darin, well, he wasn't as intense as the rest—no big goals, just taking it one day at a time.

"So, Darin, what are your thoughts after we graduate this year?" Eric asked. Wondering what he might say, all the guys had their eyes on Darin.

"Well, I think I'm going to stick around and attend the U."

This didn't surprise the group. Darin was never considered a big risk taker or adventurer. His life was basic—chock-full of homework, which he did most of the time; parties, which he occasionally attended; and the JV soccer team, on which he played second string. To his buddies he was just an average kid with average dreams. This didn't sit well with Eric, and his belly started to burn. Talking about local and average things only made Eric mad. His grandfather, his uncle, and his father had all grown up and lived in the same town, one following the other. It was clear in his mind that he wasn't going to follow those footsteps, and he didn't want any of his friends to either.

Eric finally looked up at the group and said, "Are we all just going to sit here, or are we going to make something happen with our lives? I say it's time to put up or shut up. No more talking about it, I'm ready to do something." For a moment the group sat there, looking at one another, wondering what to do or say. Inside, Sam was feeling the same way. They had spent so many nights at that table just blabbing away about what school they were going to attend, what program they would get an offer from, or what new big goal they were going to achieve. Sam had had enough as well.

"Let's do it guys," cried Sam. "Let's not let our dreams die here in this little town. Why don't we pick the one thing that each of us said we wanted and really go for it. More important, let's push one another, because that's what it's going to take!

"I'm in," said Jake. "Becky and the silver screen. Those are my goals."

"What about you, Eric. Do you want to make a Division I team or are you just talking about it?"

"I mean it." Eric said.

"What about you, Harold. Is Cal Tech really important to you?"

"Since I was a kid," he said.

Sam turned to Darin "What about you buddy: do you want to add to the pool of dreams here?"

"Of course I do! But my goals probably wouldn't interest you guys. I'll be satisfied if I get into the engineering program at the U next fall. That's what I want to do. I also want to spend more time with my family and help my little brother make it on his junior high soccer team."

The group groaned a bit. "Come on Darin," Harold said. "Isn't there something bigger that you want, something extra challenging that you want to accomplish?"

"Maybe I'm not as motivated as you guys. I'm pretty happy, actually."

"So be it," said Eric. "We love you no matter what you do. Right, boys?"

"Yeah, of course," exclaimed the rest of the pack.

The card game continued until the wee hours of the morning. Exhausted, everyone decided to call it a night, but not before the group pledged and promised to support and and push one another towards their goals.

Eric said "One year from tonight, August 21, we'll come together just like tonight and see where we are, okay?" The group consented, and before leaving, each boy wrote his goals down on a piece of parchment that Darin's sister had leftover from her art class. Eric was to be the keeper of the covenants.

School began a week later, and each of the pack began the year with a fresh look and a new vision. Eric made copies of the covenants and gave one to each boy to remind him of his commitment. It was meant to be their guiding light. But for some it became an obsession gone too far. Eric stayed after school, putting in extra hours at the weight room and on the track. Harold, taking five AP classes, was often found studying in the library until late in the night. Each week he looked more and more pale. Sam, of course, could be found at Wedgewood Country Club, where he was offered a part-time job in exchange for free tee times, range balls, and occasional lessons from the local pro, who shared in his enthusiasm for the game and for Stanford. Sam, like the rest of the pack, was rarely home. He found himself spending less and less time with his friends and his homework, blowing off the Saturday night card game at times to get in another eighteen holes. Jake, on the other hand, spent most of his after-school hours taking modeling and acting classes, using any extra time to woo his favorite girl. Weekends, as expected, were full of parties, after-game dances, and late-night movies.

On Saturday nights, you could find Darin sitting on his porch around 8:15, just waiting for his friends to show up for their card game. But for weeks, none of them showed up. Darin didn't say anything at first. He just figured that within a few weeks, everything would be back to normal and his friends would be worn out by their overzealousness. But around the sixth week, he got a bit frustrated. Where were his friends, and what were they doing?

The following Monday, Darin approached each of his buds with just one question, "What's up?" Each usually replied, "Oh, hey, Darin. Sorry about Saturday, man, but I was . . ." practicing, reading, running, attending photo shoots, or whatever goal they had that prevented their coming.

"But what about Saturday?" he then asked.

"We'll get the card game back together. Just set it up with the others, and I'll be there."

Darin made several attempts at putting together the card game, but each was fruitless. Each time he called any of his friends, he ended up talking to a frustrated parent who asked Darin what the heck was going on with his or her son. Eric's mom said, "Eric's working out in the morning, during lunch, and in the evening. I can hardly keep enough food in the house, and his school work is suffering. You're his friend, Darin. What do you think is going on?"

"An obsession for greatness, I think. But don't worry, I'll try to talk to him," Darin promised. Click.

"Sam has turned into some sort of golf nut," said his father. "I'm worried that Stanford's consumed all his thoughts. He thinks that his golf will pull him through, but what about the rest of his life?"

"I know," replied Darin. "I'll try to talk to him." Click.

Harold's house was next. Darin was shocked when Harold himself answered. "Hey, Harold, what's up? Want to hang out for a while?"

"No can do, my friend. I've got that chem exam next week, and I want to be extra prepared for it."

"But you have five more days to study, and it's only on two chapters."

"I know, I know, but I want a perfect score. Bill Stanley did that once and I'm going to match it."

"How about a card game sometime?" asked Darin. "Why don't you try to set it up and call me if it's on. Hey, got to go. Let's talk in a few days." Click.

Then came Jake's parents, who both got on the phone to find out what their son was doing spending all their money on photo shoots and clothes.

"I don't know," Darin said. "All these guys are on some sort of mission."

"Well, why don't they wake up and start thinking about other things in their lives," Jake's dad said.

"Yeah, what happened to your card games?" Jake's mom asked.

"I know, I know," said Darin, frustrated and a bit worried about his friends.

Several months later the scenario continued. Every once in a while the pack would meet for a quick lunch, see how the others were doing with their goals, and then rush off to practice, study, or whatever. Darin was proud of his friends and their dedication to the goals that they had made during that chilly August night. But how these goals became so all-consuming was beyond him.

One Friday evening after a movie with his younger brother, Darin was sitting in his room trying to come up with a plan to bring his friends back to reality, when the phone rang.

"Darin, Darin, get over here." It was Harold's mom, her voice laced with panic and desperation. "Harold's on the roof."

"What do you mean?" replied Darin.

"He's on the roof, and he won't come down. Please come over here and talk some sense into him. He said if I came out he would jump."

Darin didn't ask any more questions. He rushed to his friend's house. Mrs. Steiner, Harold's mother, had called the other pack members' houses because she thought that Harold's friends might be able to help him. Darin was the first to arrive on the scene.

Mrs. Steiner quickly told him that although Harold had prepared for months for his college entrance exams, his scores were below the average for Harvard.

Darin sprinted up the stairs to the master bedroom balcony. He peeked his head outside and scanned the rooftop looking for his frantic friend.

"What are you doing here, Darin?" Harold's voice was a raspy hiss. "Leave me alone will you? My life is over. All that work for nothing." Harold dropped his head into his hands. "I'm a loser."

"You ARE NOT a loser!" Darin said emphatically to his friend. "You're the smartest friend I've got. Now get your butt inside."

"I'm going to jump, Darin. I'm really going to do it. Head first, man. I'm done."

Darin climbed out of the window and onto the roof, moving towards Harold. Both boys heard the screeching tires and the car doors slam before they saw Eric and Sam standing on the lawn and looking up at them.

"Harold!" Sam yelled. "What's going on up there?"

Harold didn't respond. He just knelt down, rocking back and forth.

"So you'll work harder next year and get into Harvard a year later," Eric yelled up. "You can still do it, Harold."

Harold stood up and moved to the edge, refusing to talk or move from that position—until he heard another car door slam and the sobbing of Mrs. Parker, Jake's mom. This got everyone's attention, including Harold's. She explained that Jake had been in an accident on the way home from an interview. He had Becky with him, and both had been drinking. He wrapped his convertible around an oak tree only one mile away from the house. His father found them almost an hour later. Both were in rough shape, and they were rushed to the hospital.

As they all listened to Mrs. Parker, Harold seemed to snap out of his desperation for a moment to think about what might have happened to his close friend. He slowly backed away from the edge of the roof, and, although still agitated and in a panic, hobbled down the stairs, past his parents, and out onto the driveway with his friends to see Mrs. Parker and check if she was all right. Harold, Darin, Eric, and Sam jumped into Mr. Steiner's suburban and followed Jake's mother to the hospital. On the way they passed the tree, the twisted car, and the police officer taking notes in the haze of the flashing red and blue lights. After seeing the car, Harold became nauseated, and the rest of the boys stared straight ahead, wondering about the fate of their friend.

When they got to the hospital, the doctors informed the pack and their parents that Jake was in the operating room and that they were fighting for his life. Luckily, Becky, the girl he had been dating all year, came out of the wreck with only a few minor cuts and bruises. Becky told everyone that Jake was really upset that his interview didn't go well. His frustration lead to their drinking and subsequent crash.

For the boys and their parents, time inched along. Nobody knew what to expect. The boys sat together around the table in the lobby. After awhile, Darin got up and walked to the corner of the reception area. He whispered to the nurse, who left and then returned with a small package of unwrapped playing cards.

Darin returned to the table. "Ace's low or high?" he asked. The rest of his friends slowly lifted up their heads and were greeted by the happy and familiar sight of the cards.

"High," they all rumbled.

"We've had enough lows for tonight," Harold said.

"High it is." Darin dealt the cards to his friends.

"So how are you all doing? I've missed you guys the past couple months," Darin said.

"I guess we've all been doing our own thing, you know, what we talked about," replied Eric.

"Harold, you look like crap," Darin said, looking his friend in the eye. "What were you doing on that roof tonight?"

"I've had it with the intensity of it all." Harold rubbed the back of his neck. "What's the point anyway. I'm breaking my back trying to get into that freaking school, and because of it I messed up my exams. I got the worst scores of all my tests. It's all become too darned important."

"And how about you two jocks. How've you been lately?" Darin looked at Eric and Sam.

"About the same, I guess," said Eric. "I don't do much besides work out and practice, except for when Sam and I practice relaxation and mental training techniques together."

Sam nodded. "I've just been playin' golf."

Nobody said anything else about their time away from each other. They just looked at one another with guilt. But soon guilt gave way to a healthy dose of concern for their friend who was hanging between life and death. Right up there was their concern for Harold. To keep everyone optimistic, Darin kept dealing the cards, as if Jake would be coming out any minute to, as always, bluff his way to victory. The later it got, the sadder it was to see an extra hand being dealt with nobody to play it.

Forty-eight hours later, Jake's condition stabilized, and he was moved out of intensive care. Neither his parents nor Eric, Sam, Darin, or Harold left the hospital until Jake was in the clear. Harold spoke with the staff psychiatrist, but seemed to be scared straight by Jake's incident. Between the four of them, they had missed six practices, two days of studying, and one soccer game. Nobody seemed to care. In fact, it was refreshing to know that they could still work towards their goals without spending every waking minute on them.

Two weeks later, on Saturday evening, everybody showed up on time for the card game. After the first two hands, Eric stopped shuffling the cards and pulled out the parchment from last August with all their goals scrawled on it.

"I propose we amend this baby," he said.

"Agreed," Jake said. Harold seconded. Never again did these boys forget the importance of their friends and their families or the importance of living a balanced life.

Adaptations

I'm always running here and there, facing changes everywhere;
different people, uncertain scenery, odd places,
I guess these are all forms of adaptations.
As soon as I'm somewhere and everything starts to mesh,
I have to pack up and start off fresh.
It's hard to believe what this world has in store . . .
I guess if things were unchanging, life would a bore.
It seems as soon as I set my goals and high expectations,
I'm up and facing adaptations.
I can't believe some of the things I face,
you might expect I'd lose my grace;
nevertheless, I continue to stride,
for I am too strong to defeat my pride.
So I will continue to create and maintain relations;
this will certainly take time and patience . . .
this will also mean adaptations.

© Jami Lynn Bauer

Strike a good balance . . . without it you will fall.
—Amy Ripley, junior high student

Balance keeps your life on track.
—Jim Black, junior high student

Life is in harmony when life is in balance!
—Jami Lynn Bauer

My thoughts on balance

EACH OF US HAS A GENIUS

DIVERSITY

13

DIVERSITY

Each of us has a genius

In the world we live in everybody is different, and this is a wonderful thing. While many of us grow up with neighbors much like us, there are others in the world who have much to teach us. Whether white or black, Christian or Budhist, tall or short, each of us has a gift to give—a new perspective, a new way of seeing the world, a new way of thinking. Seek always to cultivate these relationships, for like traveling the world over, they will take you to places that you have never been before.

The air was starting to chill over the dark green fields of Wetherton Academy, and the trees were turning to fiery reds, earthy yellows, and dull browns. It was the kind of New England fall that you read about in English Literature class.

Josie and Liz had been at Wetherton for almost four weeks now, helping Mrs. Coniff get ready for the beginning of the field hockey season while getting an early start on their conditioning. On this particular morning, they were running some drills—long strides followed by quick shuffles—while waiting for Mrs. Coniff. They were so engrossed in their efforts that they didn't hear her approach them.

"You two just may be my starting players this year," said their coach. As she called out to them, Josie swung around startled. Then she grinned.

"What do you mean, may be your star players?" she teased.

"Well, you haven't met the new recruit then."

With a curious glare she replied, "No, no I haven't."

"I met this girl through the Leavenworth family," said Mrs. Coniff. They told me that they'd never seen such talent in an athlete and so I did a little scouting. She's quite personable. I think you girls will like her. She's different from the rest of you girls. Not from around here. It'll be interesting."

"What do you mean she's not like the rest of us?" said Liz.

"You'll see." said Coach Coniff. "Keep your eyes open. You're bound to see her at opening ceremonies next week."

"Come on, Mrs. Coniff, tell us more about her" said Josie.

"All you need to know is that she's considered one of the best field hockey players in all of New Mexico, and to top it off, she's a great student. Her name is Lucy. She won't be here until school starts, so she'll be a bit behind the rest of us. She's had some family obligations that have kept her from coming early, but she assured me she'll be ready on day one. I'm counting on you girls to take her in and get her up to speed. Now get back to work and stop asking me questions. You'll see her at the ceremonies."

Josie and Liz were quite interested in the big mystery. However, they were more focused on their training and their practices. They weren't too concerned about losing their top positions on Wetherton's famous field hockey team.

It was late afternoon during opening ceremonies when the girls and their parents met at the front gate. These twisting wrought iron gates gave the place an almost fairy-tale mystique. It was tradition for both students and their parents to ride by horse and buggy to the outdoor amphitheater.

As the crowd of girls and parents lined up by the gates, news spread in hushed whispers that some over-built Indian girl, unknown to anyone, was trying to get into a carriage, claiming to be a new student. Nobody believed her, so they didn't let her on. A Native American had never attended Wetherton before, and certainly not one measuring six feet four inches tall.

It wasn't a big deal to Lucy. She just walked—in her case strode—with everybody else who wasn't a student or a parent. Besides, it gave Lucy the opportunity to check out the statues and gaze up at the tall sandstone buildings with their regal columns covered with mature ivy and hardly legible Latin phrases. Lost in the beauty of her new school, Lucy forgot not only that was she supposed to check in, but that the ceremony was semi-formal. She wasn't wearing anything formal like most of the others, just slacks and a pullover. You could hardly help but notice her.

When she arrived at the amphitheater, Lucy noticed several eyes staring at her. She was used to this and just shrugged her shoulders. So be it. Few people could be as proud as she was of her background and heritage. When she arrived at the amphitheater, Lucy was led to her seat, next to the other "foreign" students.

Josie leaned over and tugged on Liz's collar. "That must be her!" she whispered. "That must be Lucy, Mrs. Coniff's new recruit!"

"She's a monster!" Liz laughed, but with a hint of fright.

"Yeah, but one thing's for sure," said Josie, "She could probably chew you up and spit you out inside of a New York minute."

"Ha. We'll see about that," replied Liz. A few moments passed and each kept looking over at their new teammate. Liz then piped up, "I don't care how good she is. She's not taking me down. My parents would be so embarrassed if I let an Indian girl beat me out."

"Ditto," said Josie. "I don't want to be embarrassed by her, but you heard what coach said. We just can't ignore her. We're supposed to help."

"Helping her is one thing, accepting her into the club is another!" retorted Liz. As the ceremonies commenced, both girls had a hard time keeping their eyes off their rival.

After opening ceremonies, Liz and Josie walked up to Lucy and introduced themselves politely, and their meeting was cordial. After telling Lucy that Wetherton was one of the best schools for women on the East Coast and giving a bit os its history, both girls excused themselves, feeling they had kept their end of the bargain.

"We'll get better acquainted at practice, Lucy," said Liz. "Three PM sharp tomorrow!"

Morning couldn't have come any sooner for Lucy. The sun rose, the bell tower rang, and Lucy quickly discovered that she was no longer in New Mexico. At breakfast in the cafeteria, more stares came her way, which she was used to. She then went from class to class, visited the bookstore, and toured campus without one glimpse of anyone with her same skin color. She soon felt all alone in the world. Girls stared at her, made comments behind her back, and purposely ignored her. After this long and trying first day, Lucy excitedly returned to her dorm room and turned her attention to what she wanted most to do: practice her sport. She figured that if there was anywhere that she would be accepted and respected, it would be with the field hockey team.

Practice began at 3:00 PM, but Lucy showed up at 2:15. Mrs. Coniff was sorting through the storage shed when Lucy arrived.

"Lucy!" Mrs. Coniff stopped what she was doing. "How was your first day of classes?"

"Okay, I guess. Well, actually, not that great."

Mrs. Coniff nodded. "I've seen a lot of different girls from different places come and go throughout the years. This can be a difficult place when you're not from the East."

"I can see that already," said Lucy.

"About seven years ago we had two Spanish girls here at Wetherton," Mrs. Coniff said. "They left early out of frustration. And do you know why?" Lucy shook her head. "It was because they tried to be like their peers. They tried to be something they weren't—rich, white, and ivy league. When they started acting like this, they lost all sight of who they were and their own greatness."

Coach Coniff gestured for Lucy to come closer and then whispered fiercely, "Don't forget who you are and where you come from. And most important of all, play your game!"

Lucy smiled, grabbed her stick, and began running the field just like she did back home in New Mexico. This little talk was just what she needed to boost her spirits.

At 3:00, Mrs. Coniff called the girls together and welcomed them to their first official practice. "Welcome, girls. We are excited to be together as a team again. It's been a while since many of us have been together. But before we get into the gossip, I want you all to meet our newest player, Lucy. She's one of the finest players to come out of New Mexico, and I'm excited that she has chosen Wetherton as her home for the next few years." A few girls clapped slightly and gave a couple cheers, but only because it was expected of them. When the announcements were over, all the girls were instructed to break up into pairs. Lucy looked at Coach Coniff, who could see the determination in Lucy's eyes.

As one of the last pairs to form, Lucy ended up with one of the other new recruits, a rather shy girl named Gina, who didn't attract much attention. This unlikely pair looked at one another, consented, and ran out with everybody else. Working harder than anybody on the field, the two girls out-sprinted and out-stickhandled the other girls. Practice became a little tougher today. A new standard had been introduced. By the end of the afternoon, the others began to mix their resentment with a smidgen of respect.

Off the field, Lucy's classes continued to produce moments of insecurity and sensitivity, especially in her American history class where the acts of the American Indians were often debated.

On discussing the discovery of the Americas, Lucy had a different view. "But Dr. Dunboro," Lucy called out, "Columbus and other explorers of his day brought disease, stole lands, and managed to destroy many people for the sake of personal gain and profit. How do you feel about that?"

Josie watched with some admiration as Lucy argued with the toughest teacher on campus. Dr. Dunboro was known for his sharp intellect and keen sense of power in his classes and lectures. But Lucy knew her stuff, especially her Native American history. In fact, for her oral presentation on the Navajo tribe, of which she was a member, Lucy added a bit of color by wearing a magnificently beaded Indian dress, discussing some of the tales and folklore behind it. Lucy captivated everyone in her class for nearly forty-five minutes. Each student, including Josie, walked away not only with some interesting information, but also with a real appreciation for the beauty and content of her message. Mr. Dunboro gave her one of the highest grades in the class, and deservedly so. Everyone was becoming used to Lucy and her unique characteristics—and most importantly, liking her for them.

Back on the field, Lucy continued to show her stuff. At every practice she worked harder than any of the other girls, did what Coach Coniff instructed her to do, and helped her teammates whenever possible, often sacrificing her time on the field so that rookies could develop their games. By popular vote, Lucy was considered to be one of the top three players on the team, along with Josie and Liz.

As the season progressed, Lucy and the rest of the team were ecstatic about their results: 11 and 1 in their division. Their only loss was, of course, to Pinehurst. But they had one more chance to avenge their loss—at the next invitational.

Since their big loss, practice time had almost doubled. Everyone was up at sunrise to participate in team aerobic training and returned in the afternoons for drills, weight training, and discussions on strategy. The team did everything together. They ate, worked out, practiced, studied, and spent their free time together. In essence, they were a single unit with a common goal. They were ready once again for the challenge that lay before them—Pinehurst.

The night before they were scheduled to leave for the invitational, Mrs. Coniff pulled her team together for a talk. After discussing strategy and giving her usual pep talk, Mrs. Coniff ended by saying, "You've come a long way, girls. I'm proud of you. I know it's hard, but don't worry so much about winning or losing. The way you all have trained, I know you are the best team on the Eastern Seaboard. Just do your best and everything will turn out as it should." This seemed pointed enough. The girls let out whoops and hollers, and then Lucy stood up.

"I'd like to quickly say something, if that's okay." Mrs. Coniff and the rest of the team nodded. Lucy then gathered her thoughts for a moment. "You know, we've come a long way over the last several months, not only as a team, but also individually. I can't believe all that I've experienced in such a short time. I know it's been difficult for all of you to get used to me. I come from a different world, one where only a handful of kids have enough money to go to a good school like this. I just wanted to thank you for giving me a chance to be part of this team. I've tried to do my best for you, to be your teammate and friend. And I hope you realize that there isn't anything I wouldn't do for you. So if I may say, let's commit ourselves now to going the extra mile and delivering a victory for Coach Coniff!" As Lucy stepped back into the circle of athletes, warm hands covered her back. But she was not finished. "Oh, and one last thing. Could everyone meet me at 10:00 PM tonight at the fire pits? I have got something special I want to share with all of you."

Looking a bit confused, they all nevertheless seemed intrigued by this request and nodded in consent. They had done everything else together, why not tonight.

At 9:50, most of the girls started to show up, only to be met by a strange sight reflected by a strange light. Lucy was standing by a roaring fire, wearing some type of ceremonial Indian dress. As the girls began to surround the fire, Lucy kept silent, motioned for them to do the same, and continued to tend the fire. By 10:05, every member of the team had made it to the pit. All were silent, yet looking at one another with curiosity, until finally overcome by the hypnotic nature of the fire. Lucy then stood before them, staring deeply into the flames. She then looked squarely in the eyes of her teammates.

"I want to share something with you," she said, "something that you've probably never seen before." In her mind, she silently added, "And probably something you never would have accepted a few months ago."

"I'd like to lead you in a special dance," she continued, "one that will give us good luck in tomorrow's tournament." Lucy looked around the circle at her teammates, who were all wide-eyed and curious. Seeing the readiness on her teammates' faces, she turned around and switched on her small portable stereo. Beating drums engulfed them. Lucy started making movement to the sounds. She began dancing around the fire, pulling each of the girls in with her. Josie and Liz were slightly more reserved, but soon the whole team, including Josie and Liz, were twisting and dancing, each freely expressing themselves as they had never done before. It was a safe place.

The girls danced for nearly an hour, until, exhausted and exhilarated, they came together for the close of their evening. They ended it as they had begun it—in silence, looking at one another. They knew they would never forget the experience they had had that evening.

Needless to say, nobody had seen Wetherton play with such passion and commitment as they did the next day. You might guess who won the game that day. Pinehurst didn't know what hit them. Each Wetherton girl walked away from the game more physically and emotionally fit—even spiritually fit—than ever before. But more important than this was their appreciation and love for each other.

As the girls got into the school vans to head back to Wetherton, both Liz and Josie approached Lucy, slipped an arm over her shoulders, and said: "Do you have a victory dance for us too?" All Lucy could do was smile.

Stereotype

They don't even know you,
yet they call you by name.
You see, it's quite simple . . .
It's a societal game;
They can't see what's within
because they're living without
They'll be quick to put a
label on you without a doubt.
It's an easy alibi, yet such
a shame . . . they don't even
know you . . .
yet they call you by name.

© Jami Lynn Bauer

It's amazing what you can learn from someone who is different than you.
—Robin Spencer, eighth grade

The world is a better place because of our differences.
—Brock Argon, eighth grade

We are a nation of communities, of tens and tens of thousands of ethnic, religious, social, business, labor union, neighborhood, regional and other organizations, all of them varied, voluntary, and unique . . . a brilliant diversity spread like stars, like a thousand points of light in a broad and peaceful sky.
—President George H. W. Bush (#41)

My thoughts on diversity

YOU ARE ONLY AS STRONG
AS YOUR WEAKEST LINK

TEAMWORK

14

TEAMWORK

You are only as strong as your weakest link

No matter what you do in life, being a team player is critical for your success. Even if you play a game alone, there are many who support and sustain you. Whether these are teammates, friends, or family, there are many who will have made you who you are. Pay attention to their contributions, pay attention to your contributions to others, and remember that we are together in this game we call life.

Jenny was twelve years old when she saw her first basketball game. It was a game for her brother's high school team, which he had finally made after being cut for two years in a row. It was only minutes into the game, and, like her brother, Jenny was hooked. It was all so exciting, players running up and down the court fighting for the ball. There was so much action that Jenny was at the edge of her seat the whole time. At that moment she knew that she too wanted to play basketball, just like her older brother.

Jenny's parents were thrilled with their daughter's interest in basketball. They bought her a ball and hoop of her own, placed them in the basement, and watched as Jenny hopped around attempting to sink shots from all corners of the room.

Jenny's brother, Peter, was as helpful as he could be. He showed her all the moves he had learned himself, which were only a few, but enough to capture her attention. Although there wasn't much talent in the young girl, it wasn't long before Jenny wanted to be on a team of her own. Her goal: to make the junior high girls basketball team.

For being such a small town, Farmington had one heck of a basketball team. The auditorium was always filled with screaming family and friends who were loyal to the team. It was a bit intimidating for Jenny, but she was excited to give it a try.

The coach took an instant liking to Jenny and invited her to practice with the team. Knowing that she didn't have much experience, Jenny didn't expect to be a starter. Instead, she just wanted to have the opportunity to practice, hang around new people, and be part of the action. The only problem: Jenny wasn't very good, and everybody let her know it.

Little slack was given to the newly turned thirteen-year-old. At practice she was attentive and eager but often made drilling errors that interrupted the team's workout. Jenny was quickly pegged as a klutz, often dropping the ball when it was her turn to give or receive a pass. In the locker room after practice, Jenny usually received the cold shoulder from her teammates. The girls weren't very nice to her, and it wasn't long before she started to lose confidence in herself. One day after a scrimmage game, two girls came into the locker room, walked over to where Jenny was sitting, and told her that she should quit the team and stop making problems for everybody. They even made a threat or two. This discouraged Jenny quite a bit, and she didn't know what to do. Her love of the game started to dwindle, and her thoughts of quitting were never far off. Then one day it all changed.

After several weeks of subtle abuse, Jenny, while participating in a passing exercise, fumbled the ball so badly that she thought she would never hear the end of it. While some of the girls were ready to dig into her, a lone teammate, whom she hardly knew, stepped in and said something that nobody had yet said to her. Instead of the usual "stupid" or "clumsy," Jenny heard somebody say, "That's all right, you'll get it." These were just a few brief words, but they brought such comfort to her she could hardly believe it.

The girl who came to her rescue was Tina, a rather tall girl who had been playing on the girls team since the year before. A transfer student from another school and considered one of the better players on the team, Tina couldn't stand to hear her teammates treat Jenny like they had been doing over the past several weeks. In fact, Tina had been putting up with this kind of behavior since she made the team and just couldn't take it any more. Instead of chastising Jenny for her mistakes, Tina took it upon herself to see what she could do to help her and a few other girls who were also struggling.

Since practice had started more than a month earlier, the Scorpions hadn't played well in many of the scrimmage games. There was too much opposition and too much ball hogging and selfish behavior, the stuff that tears teams apart rather than brings them together. Tina knew that if the Scorpions were to live up to their reputation, something had to be done about this team or it would quickly self-destruct.

At practice Tina made it a point to compliment Jenny on everything she did well. When other teammates criticized Jenny, or any other girl for that matter, Tina was the first to back Jenny up, pointing out to the rest of her teammates that being part of the problem was easy, but being part of the solution was what they needed.

During the team's difficulties, rather than take matters into her own hands, the Scorpions' coach stood by to see how her team would come together. She hoped that their difficulties wouldn't be so bad that she would have to intervene. She trusted the evolution that most successful teams go through. Noticing the lead that Tina took to help Jenny, coach Thompson simply watched as her girls began taking some of the heat off the poor performers on the team, especially Jenny, who probably suffered the most. Instead of criticizing her, more of the players began helping her and giving her advice. It wasn't long before Jenny and others were feeling better about themselves, about the game, and about the team.

The mood and energy began to change at every practice. Instead of looking at who made what mistake, the girls began to realize that their chain was only as strong as its weakest link. And while they had several links that could break the chain, nobody wanted to be part of an unsuccessful, if not downright hostile, team. It didn't take long for attitudes to change. Instead of taunting and ridiculing the weakest players, Tina and the other girls began taking the time to support, coach, and befriend them. Soon everyone was becoming closer, and they were having a lot more fun.

While practices were becoming more fun and more productive, the team began to feel a sense of unity. Like an orchestra with all of the instruments playing in perfect harmony, this girls basketball team began to recognize the importance of teamwork, of caring for one another, and that being divided was destructive. They chose to come together.

Through the rest of their season together, the Scorpions kept their loyal crowd; won the majority of their games and tournaments; and made sure that everyone had the chance to play, learn, grow, and win. This set a precedent, as the rookie players just recruited would be leading the team over the next several seasons, recognizing the inherent value of teamwork and their ability to achieve—together.

True Champions

A **together** team—no matter what happens,
it's clear to see that we are **true** champions.
Winning together, losing together,
forever showing respect and admiration—
this is what real winning is about.
Team spirit, friendship, laughter, and fun—
our team posesses all of these things . . .
and no matter what the score,
in our eyes
we
have won.

© Jami Lynn Bauer

There is no I in teamwork!
—Courtney Kolb, junior high student

Teamwork + Togetherness = Achieve More
—Jim Black, junior high student

The human contribution is the essential ingredient. It is only in the giving of oneself to others that we truly live.
—Ethel Percy Andrus

My thoughts on teamwork

MOVING IN THE DIRECTION
OF YOUR DREAMS

REFINEMENT

15

REFINEMENT

Moving in the direction of your dreams

Remember that your adventures on and off the playing field will come and go. New fields await you, and new opportunities will arrive every month and every year. You will enter many stages of life—each quite different from the next. With these stages come many changes and many new challenges. To meet these challenges you must remember where you came from and where you are going. Make sure to review your goals regularly and reflect what you have learned during each season of your life; use each stage as a platform to prepare you for bigger and better games of life.

As he walked down the stairs, Adam pulled his sticky shirt away from his chest. It was blistering hot when the air conditioner whirred, sputtered, then died. With his parents gone until tomorrow morning, Adam had all the time in the world to be by himself and reflect on what had taken place over the last seventeen years of his life. As the brilliant sun was setting, Adam headed for the porch, where there was at least a chance of a light breeze.

Adam sank onto the soft cushions of the porch sofa and folded his arms behind his head. "It's all good," he thought. "My life is all good." His senior year of high school was over, and it had been a month now since his last graduation party. Most of the boys had left the show, on to bigger and better places, to public and private colleges and universities all over the country. And in a few days it would be his turn.

Adam looked out at the front yard. The dark shapes of the trees stretched up toward the stars. He could hear the rustling of the leaves as the wind stirred. It didn't seem that long ago that those trees had been much smaller. "This is where it all started," Adam thought. In this front yard he had caught his first football with his dad, hit his first baseball with Billy, and had wrestled his first match with Chip.

Even more memorable were the times he walked around the neighborhood with his father, just talking about anything. Adam attributed most everything that he had learned to his family and to the fields on which he had played.

He wasn't the first in his family to play on this front lawn and other great fields. Adam's grandfather had played for the New York Yankees; Aunt Jane competed as a swimmer in the 1976 Olympic Games; and both his father, Jerry, and brother, Billy, were all-American football players. Dad, or "Flash," as his buddies called him, was a linebacker for Florida State. Billy, following in his father's footsteps, was just beginning his second year at his father's alma mater. Adam was a gifted athlete also, but his dream was one of medicine, not of professional athletics.

Adam pulled his chair closer to the porch railing so he could prop his feet up. He remembered when he was fourteen and had sat with his father in this very chair to discuss life and receive an earful of advice. He could still remember his father handing over that faded brown notebook, saying, "Son, I want you to write down what's most important to you." Adam pictured his skinny frame hunched over the notebook, writing things about God, family, friends, and everything he wanted in life.

Adam rubbed his hand against his chin, trying to remember the old list. As he started thinking about his past heroes, he remembered more and more about the people he admired and their qualities that he wanted to develop. Next to John Wayne he had written "confident"; for Einstein, "creative"; for Charlie Chaplin, "humorous"; Dad, "strong"; Billy, "committed"; Mom, "organized"; and Beth, "driven." Then there were the goals he had set for himself for football, track, school, finances, and college.

As he reviewed the old notebook in his mind, Adam jumped out of his seat, ran up to his bedroom, and pulled open his bottom desk drawer. He rummaged through old papers, pictures, and other junk until he found the original list he was pondering. Adam smoothed the notebook's crumpled sheets of paper and examined the contents as he descended the staircase, back into the night's heat and the sounds of crickets. As he rummaged through the papers, Adam grinned as he realized that he had reached all but one of his goals. His only miss was running a 4:30 mile in track. He was off by only 6 seconds. Adam placed the list next to him on the brightly flowered cushions and stared at the night sky with a sense of quiet satisfaction.

Suddenly this satisfaction was replaced by an empty feeling inside. "It's all over," he thought to himself. "The goals, the experiences, the freedoms of high school. It's all over." It seemed strange that although he felt peaceful and happy about achieving his goals, a sense of fear stood right behind the happiness. Everything until this time had been planned out. He knew exactly what to do, but now the doing was over. He had become all that he wanted and had refined himself to be like the many people whom he had admired. What now?

Before dwelling too long on the past, Adam remembered that his quest for greatness did not have to end here. He had yet to refine and develop himself to the next level and chapter of his life. It was time to celebrate his accomplishments while recommitting himself to an even greater path.

Adam filled a tall glass of lemonade, found the most comfortable position he could, grabbed a pen, turned to a fresh section of the notebook, and began writing. With new and inspired images, Adam sat under the yellow porch light pondering his future development and setting new goals. They included completing college in the top ten percent of his class, getting into medical school, becomming an all-American, meeting the girl of his dreams, and joining a fraternity.

Adam then decided to look at what kind of person he had become and who had shaped his life. He was grateful that he had patterned his life after so many people that he admired. Now he had the opportunity to create a new list, one also derived from those whom he knew and respected—people he wanted to be more like: there was Coach Eddings, who taught him about perseverance and strategy and his science teacher, Mrs. Madison, who had introduced him to the beauty and appreciation of nature. Adam continued thinking of those who had shaped his life; just as with his previous list of heroes and their qualities, he wrote down their names first followed by the quality or behavior he wanted to develop. These people were added to guide and refine him yet further towards the person he wanted to become.

Adam ignored the tightness in his neck and instead flipped to another page, where he began listing the steps he could now take to move toward his newly articulated goals and qualities. As he brought his hand atop his head, he realized that he had not moved for hours.

When the grandfather clock inside the hallway chimed two o'clock in the morning, Adam closed the notebook, smoothing its tattered cover. He unfolded himself, stretched a bit, and climbed the stairs slowly, smiling.

As Adam put the notebook back into his desk drawer, he noticed a familiar quote scratched into the cover in faint pencil. "If I were given seven hours to chop down a tree, I'd spend five of those hours sharpening my saw."

When Adam's head hit his pillow, he was satisfied with his progress and his new quest for greatness. He brought to a close a great high school career and set his sights on an even greater journey ahead. His direction was clear. He had it down on paper, and in a few more years, he would sharpen his saw and measure his goals once again!

Jigsaw Puzzle

It's the end of the day
and I'm lying in bed
I analyze what I've done
and even what I've said.
Trying to put life into perspective
is a daily chore—
some days seem harder to bear.
It's as though life is a
giant jigsaw puzzle
Each day we try to piece it together
in hopes of creating a whole.
Sometimes we add a piece
that simply does not fit
Only to realize that others
could mesh better
This is why we don't quit.
Similar to the mis-fits
are the mistakes we make in life
Patience, persistence, perspective
We can piece it together
if we try.

© Jami Lynn Bauer

Fine tuning even the simplest of skills will make me a better athlete.
—Brian Lender, eighth grade

Goals aren't something you set just once.
—Trevor Gibb, seventh grade

[Sharpening the saw] is the single most powerful investment we can ever make in life—investment in ourselves, in the only instrument we have with which to deal with life and to contribute. We are the instruments of our own performance, and to be effective, we need to recognize the importance of taking time regularly to sharpen the saw.
—Stephen R. Covey, author of *The 7 Habits of Highly Effective People*

My thoughts on refinement

CONCLUSION

Before you close the covers of this book, ponder once again the qualities you've read about. Remember your thoughts and feelings as you've journeyed within.

Always remember that you are the master of your own fate. You, and only you, have the power to choose who you wish to become. It has been said that you are the sum total of what you think about most. Keep this thought in mind as you ponder the future you.

Sports, like life, are an adventure. Life is a game where rules apply and winners prevail. While you will experience many games in your life, remember what you've experienced here. Seek to apply each quality within the games of your life, and as you master the understanding that the only thing you can control is yourself, you will realize that no matter what happens, winning is always within your grasp!

ABOUT THE WRITERS AND DESIGNERS

Dr. Bruce H. Jackson

As a practitioner and student of applied human performance technologies, Dr. Jackson is dedicated to the ongoing development of individuals, teams, and organizations.

Searching for the common denominators of performance, Dr. Jackson has worked with young athletes, inner-city children, and Fortune 500 companies alike—recognizing that the principles of personal excellence and performance are as valid for the aspiring student as well as the well-established CEO.

Dr. Jackson is a certified member of the United States Professional Tennis Association and Professional Ski Instructors of America. He holds a Master's degree in Counseling Psychology from the Boston University School of Education, a Master's degree in Business Administration from the University of Minnesota Carlson School of Management, a third Master's degree in Organizational Development from The Fielding Graduate University, and a Ph.D. in Human and Organizational Systems from the Fielding Graduate University where his research identifies many of the core components and strategies that people use to search for and replicate their "peak experiences."

Dr. Jackson currently serves as the Director for The Center for the Advancement of Leadership at Utah Valley State University—a leading organization in the study and practice of youth and adult leadership development. He also directs the C. Charles Jackson Foundation whose focus is to promote leadership, character, and life-skills development for youth throughout the U.S. In addition, Dr. Jackson also serves as the CEO of The Institute of Applied Human Excellence, a training firm dedicated to helping individuals, teams, and organizations find their peak performances through flow.

As writer, speaker, author, consultant, coach, and leadership adventure facilitator, Dr. Jackson's core interests are to help individuals seek their highest capacities while fulfilling meaningful life missions.

Dr. Jackson and his wife, Marta, with son's, Blake, and Lucas, currently live in Highland, Utah.

JAMI L. BAUER is a teacher, writer, published poet, and tennis coach. She received the Editor's Choice Award from the National Library of Poetry and the Target Teacher's Scholarship Award. She is a member of the Loft Literary Center in Minneapolis. Jami is also a certified tennis professional and a member of the United States Professional Tennis Association. She is finishing her master's degree in education with a core study in learning disabilities. She believes valuable lessons are learned in all arenas of life, especially those of sport and play. She resides in St. Paul, Minnesota, and is the proud mother of two (Gabriel and Willow).

KITTY WONG, born in Hawaii, works in the fields of illustration and graphic design. With her strong portfolio, she obtains many international freelance jobs designing logos and doing Web design. To contact Kitty please email her at kittydesign@hotmail.com

MERRILEE LIDDIARD lives in New York City with her husband Jon Douglas Liddiard. She graduated from Brigham Young University with a BFA in illustration. Merrilee has illustrated for several magazines, newpapers, and literary journals such as *Insight, Inscape Magazine,* the *Bullhorn, Slug,* and others. She has also been featured in *Spectrum Annual 9* and *CMYK* magazine.

CPSIA information can be obtained at www.ICGtesting.com
Printed in the USA
LVOW10s0027270914

406123LV00001B/54/P

9 781608 446797